THE WYCKOFF METHOD 2022

How to make profits in the financial market. Discover how Technical Analysis can help you anticipate market moves and become a profitable trader

© **Copyright 2022 - All rights reserved**.

This document is geared towards providing exact and reliable information in regard to the topic and issue covered.

- From a Declaration of Principles which was accepted and approved equally by a Committee of the American Bar Association and a Committee of Publishers and Associations.

In no way is it legal to reproduce, duplicate, or transmit any part of this document in either electronic means or in printed format. All rights reserved.

The information provided herein is stated to be truthful and consistent, in that any liability, in terms of inattention or otherwise, by any usage or abuse of any policies, processes, or directions contained within is the solitary and utter responsibility of the recipient reader. Under no circumstances will any legal responsibility or blame be held against the publisher for any reparation, damages, or monetary loss due to the information herein, either directly or indirectly.

Respective authors own all copyrights not held by the publisher.

The information herein is offered for informational purposes solely and is universal as so. The presentation of the information is without contract or any type of guarantee assurance.

The trademarks that are used are without any consent, and the publication of the trademark is without permission or backing by the trademark owner. All trademarks and brands within this book are for clarifying purposes only and are owned by the owners themselves, not affiliated with this document.

Table of Contents

Introduction

CHAPTER 1: **THE WYCKOFF METHOD**

    Stock Selection

CHAPTER 2: **THE FIVE-STEP APPROACH TO THE MARKET**

CHAPTER 3: **WYCKOFF'S "COMPOSITE MAN"**

CHAPTER 4: **THREE WYCKOFF LAWS**

CHAPTER 5: **WYCKOFF PRICE CYCLE IN DEPTH**

CHAPTER 6: **WYCKOFF PHASES/EVENTS: ACCUMULATION AND DISTRIBUTION**

    Small Orders
    Spread Betting
    Moving Averages
    Stop-Loss Systems
    Technical Analysis
    Fundamental Analysis
    Consistent Price Movement
    Reversal Points
    Insider Trading

CHAPTER 7: **HOW MARKETS MOVE**

    How Markets Move: A Historical Perspective
    How to Use the Method?
    The Problem with Trend Following
    What About Trend-Following Trading?

CHAPTER 8: **CAN RETAIL TRADERS ACTUALLY MOVE THE MARKET?**

CHAPTER 9: **SUPPLY AND DEMAND ANALYSIS**

CHAPTER 10: **COMPARATIVE STRENGTH ANALYSIS**

CHAPTER 11: **WYCKOFF GRAPHS EXPLAINED**

What Does It Take to Study Wyckoff Indicators?
What You Can Do with the Wyckoff Method of Investing

CHAPTER 12: 3 FUNDAMENTAL LAWS

CHAPTER 13: HOW TO TRADE APPLYING THE WYCKOFF METHODOLOGY—MADE EASY

For Trend Trading
For Counter-Trend Trading
For Trend Trading Using the Wyckoff Method
For Counter-Trend Trading Using the Wyckoff Method

CHAPTER 14: HOW TO TRADE AND INVEST IN STOCKS AND BONDS

Bonds Issued by Companies

CHAPTER 15: CORRELATION BETWEEN THE WYCKOFF METHODOLOGY AND REAL ESTATE MARKET TRENDS

CONCLUSION

Introduction

Investors often find Wyckoff Method difficult to grasp, but it effectively analyzes the market. We'll take a look at its history and how it can help investors avoid horrendous losses by spotting divergences in stock prices.

The Wyckoff Method is a form of technical analysis that was first developed by Richard D. Wyckoff in the early twentieth century. The method uses price charts to identify trends, support and resistance levels, trading signals, and other technical indicators that are considered predictive for future price action.

The Wyckoff Method is based on natural law and human behavior theory, which suggests that all action follows a predictable pattern. The method uses these principles to help investors spot points of overbought and oversold conditions in the market. It also helps identify areas where a stock may be vulnerable to large price fluctuations and volatile price charts.

Richard D. Wyckoff first used the Wyckoff Method as a trader on the floor of the New York Stock Exchange in 1917. While a clerk on the floor of the NYSE, Wyckoff realized an opportunity to capitalize on trading patterns. He eventually took a position as a trading advisor and rose to the senior trade desk by 1923.

Wyckoff began publishing articles on technical analysis of the financial markets in the journal "Cincinnatus" from 1924 to 1938. His first book, "Technical Analysis of Stock Trends," was published in 1934 and became a classic of technical analysis.

In 1959, Wyckoff remained faithful to his original teachings after he retired from the NYSE floor. He published a revised edition of "Technical Analysis of Stock Trends," which is now known as "New Day for Technical Traders."

The methodology behind the Wyckoff Method is simple, but it can be difficult to apply to technical analysis. The idea behind the method is that every market participant follows a set of rules in making trading decisions. Human behavior is predictable, and investors are naturally drawn to patterns that mimic their own personal desires. As long as the end result is similar, we tend to follow those patterns regardless of how we got there. We then tend to blame our fate on the markets rather than on our end-of-the-day actions and decisions on which we can realistically control and influence.

Wyckoff believed that all market participants have a set of fixed rules that they follow in making trading decisions. These rules are established by personal characteristics and the age at which the investor was first exposed to trading techniques. These characteristics include:

- Ability – The ability to instinctively understand market patterns and techniques is a skill that only a few investors possess. The more experienced you become, the more difficult it is to interpret price movements or skew market signals. This inability to read price patterns has been referred to as "chart illiteracy" by some analysts and traders.
- Experience – The Wyckoff Method is a very effective way of identifying trading signals when market participants have limited experience. As a rule, less experienced traders utilize price patterns that they unconsciously recognize in their own trading approach. These patterns are often recognizable by inexperienced traders, but they also tend to be confirmed in the charts of more experienced investors.
- Confidence – The ability to interpret price movements is enhanced when investors have a greater degree of confidence in the markets and the stock exchange in which they trade. A sudden change in market sentiment or a bullish breakout tends to be confirmed by more confident traders who follow their own rules and strategies for making decisions.
- Emotion – Emotion plays a significant role in the interpretation of price charts because it clouds the ability to make analytical decisions in the market. When investors are fearful, they tend to

make decisions based on their own personal situations rather than on the merits of the situation in which they find themselves.

Chapter 1: The Wyckoff Method

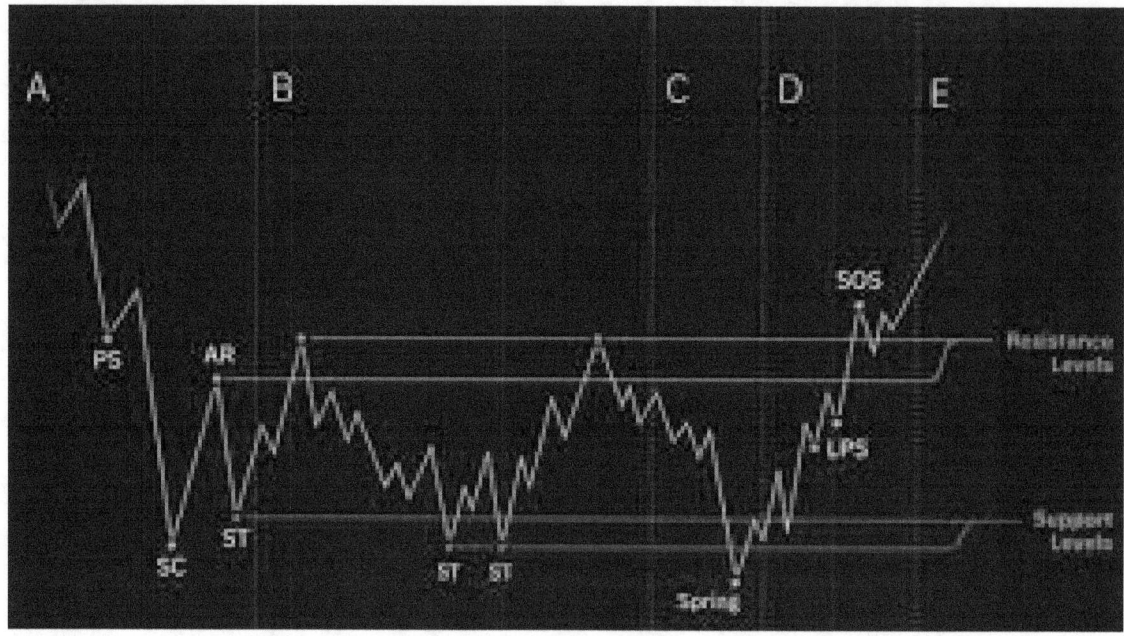

The Wyckoff Method is a simple, straightforward approach to stock trading that has been used by generations of traders. The name "Wyckoff" comes from Richard Wyckoff, who was one of the foremost authorities on price behavior in the early 20th century.

Though it's not complicated because it focuses on fundamentals and tries to draw reasonable conclusions about what will happen next, the Wyckoff Method is one of the most widely used methods for analyzing financial markets. It takes a lot of study and practice to become proficient at using this method, but once you have mastered it, you'll be able to make profitable trades because you'll know what stocks are worth purchasing or selling.

The Wyckoff Method is based on the idea that all markets, including stocks and commodities markets, exhibit cyclical behavior. Trends can be either up or down with higher highs and higher lows as price moves in the direction of the trend. Support and resistance levels are identified as price movements reach levels where there is a large buildup of supply or demand. Trend lines drawn on a chart to connect these highs and lows can be used to predict future price targets.

The Wyckoff method applies technical analysis that tries to interpret market and stock behavior based on historical precedent (e.g., factoring in how prices have changed over time). The method uses indicators to identify trends and chart patterns. Wyckoff practitioners use these charts to predict future price movements. Traders can use the Wyckoff method for securities trading, futures trading, options trading, energy trading, investment analysis, and any securities-related activities.

The Wyckoff Method is complex, and there are many techniques that must be mastered before you can profit from it. Many traders using this method also rely on other systems such as Elliott Wave analysis or Candlestick mentality to make sure they aren't making mistakes when using the Wyckoff Method.

Richard Wyckoff developed a systematic approach to trading stocks that is still used today by many traders. He put together a book that described what he did and how he did it called "Trading in the Stock Market." In this collection of books, he emphasized the importance of watching volume and price movements, understanding market psychology and using technical analysis to make trading decisions.

One of his students was Jesse Livermore, who became one of the most famous traders in history. Jesse Livermore stated, "I am indebted to Richard Wyckoff for my start in analysis, and I regard what I know about the stock market as due principally to his influence." He wrote the book "Reminiscences of a Stock Operator," even though it contained only the second half of his life. The first half of his life, he had spent trading in stocks, commodities, and bonds.

Jesse Livermore was known for using the so-called "Livermore" method, where he used very simple mathematical formulas to help him make his trading decisions. He also adapted the so-called "Livermore Method" to the Wyckoff Method. He became one of the most successful traders in history by applying these methods to trades in stocks and commodities.

What he did was he identified the trend before entering a trade, then made sure to adopt a position that would take advantage of the trend, and finally exit the position after the trend changed direction. Many people have followed his example by using this method to trade stocks. By following these steps, you can also become successful at trading.

These are some of the basic elements that are used by the Wyckoff Method:

We recommend that you learn these methods first before proceeding with this method. Some people may use other systems together with the Wyckoff Method for better results.

Every market goes through cyclical behavior, which can be either up or down, though there are always corrections along the way. These cyclical movements can be analyzed and interpreted by using indicators to identify trends and chart patterns. The Wyckoff Method uses two types of technical analysis:

The Wyckoff Method looks at stocks according to their fundamental value. Left-side up and right-side down charts are the most common indicators used by traders who use the method.

Both EMA and MACD can give you a good idea about where a stock that has been trading is likely to stop moving in the future. You can use these indicators in conjunction with the prevailing trend to predict future price movement.

If you're using the Wyckoff Method, you may also be following other systems such as Elliott Wave or candlestick mentality to ensure that your signals are reliable.

The Wyckoff Method is a simple approach to measuring value when identifying trends in the stock market. Some people prefer to use more complex systems when analyzing stocks. There are many different methods for analyzing stocks, but you'll most likely have to learn more than one method if they are different enough that you want them to complement each other. We recommend that you learn the Wyckoff Method first before using other systems.

Technical analysis is a method of determining value in financial markets by studying market charts. Patterns in market behavior are detected, interpreted, and used to form trading strategies. This method has its roots in ancient times when traders marked down their observations on scrolls of paper. The oldest known technical analysis book was written in China over 2,000 years ago. It was called "The Book of Changes" or "I Ching" by its Chinese name. Since then, the book has been translated into many languages, including English, and it's still widely read today.

There are two types of technical analysis: fundamental and technical. Fundamental analysis is something that involves analyzing a company's income statement, balance sheet, and other financial data. Technical analysis is focused on studying market behavior to predict future price movements.

In the Wyckoff method, the following factors must be considered before making a trading decision:

If you can absorb these elements into your trading process, it will help you establish a solid methodology to use when making trading decisions. Suppose you learn the Wyckoff method first and build up your trading strategy from there. In that case, it will be much easier for you to understand what's going on in the market while also being able to predict future price movements with a high degree of accuracy.

The Wyckoff Method is a great place to start when learning how to trade. This method is very intuitive for people interested in the stock market, which makes it one of the most approachable methods for understanding how the stock market works.

There are many different trading strategies that you can develop when you use the most important elements of the Wyckoff Method. Many people have made a lot of money by learning how to use these factors to help them make good trades in the market.

A lot of traders don't have any background in technical analysis, but they can still benefit from using it. If you're an expert in technical analysis, then it's easy for you to apply your knowledge when using this method.

Technical analysis is a very powerful tool that can be used in combination with fundamental analysis when making trading decisions. Technical factors can be used to calculate the probability of future price movement.

There are some other elements that you can use in conjunction with the Wyckoff Method. You may consider using some other technical indicators such as:

You may also want to analyze your trading performance through a financial tool such as:

If you're interested in starting trading, then you should start by learning the basics. There are many trading systems out there that will teach you all of these things. You can go on and learn other methods later on if you like and make sure to use them along with this method for a more effective and profitable strategy.

There are some things to consider when using this method. Some people ask whether it's possible to locate the bottoms on the left side of a chart or on the right side, but they're both just part of the same process of finding value in stocks. The method is designed to identify price movements, but it doesn't matter which direction they happen in. If you want to find out where a stock is likely to reverse course, then look for instances where prices are moving up slowly and are gradually moving down again, which means there is probably another correction coming along soon.

Another thing that many people don't like about the Wyckoff Method is the fact that it doesn't work well on some volatile stocks. If you can't handle an increase in volatility in your trading, then you should probably stick to a more conservative approach.

Many traders also don't like the fact that there's no way to know what pattern will happen next. The method is based largely on pattern recognition, so if you're looking for patterns to predict future events, then it's best to learn as many technical charting methods as possible and combine them with your own creativity and intuition.

Many successful stock traders have used the Wyckoff Method over the years.

Some of the most famous investors, including Jesse Livermore, Bernard Baruch, William J. O'Neil, Charles Dow, and Richard W. Schabacker, have all written books or taught courses about this method because they know how powerful it is.

The Wyckoff Method has been around for a long time, so there are many different types of resources you can use to learn it.

Much of what you learn when using the Wyckoff Method is based on pattern recognition. If you can learn how to use pattern recognition effectively, it will be easier for you to develop more profitable trades. Many people who don't know the Wyckoff Method often come up with their own pattern recognition methods, but they're usually not as effective as the method itself.

You may also want to learn about some other technical indicators. There are a variety of tools you can use to analyze your trading performance. It's important to be able to make a profit regardless of what happens around the market. This is why it's important that you learn as many different methods as possible and incorporate them all into your strategy if they make sense of your investment style.

Once you've mastered the basic elements, then you should start exploring other strategies to enhance your trading results.

You may want to consider a system that includes a combination of technical analysis, fundamental analysis, and rule-based strategies. A good example of a system like this is the Dow Theory.

There are many different methods that use patterns and charting, but none of them are as effective as using the Wyckoff Method itself. The vast majority of these systems aren't as reliable because they don't use proper scientific principles to make predictions about future price movements.

There are many different charting methods you can use, along with the Wyckoff Method, both on the technical side and the fundamental side. You may want to look into trading methods that are based on individual stocks

Another thing you can do is use some other financial tools for your analysis and trading decisions. Some of the most useful ones are person-to-person sites, blogs, newsletters, and forums.

There are some things you can do to develop your trading skills even more. If you're interested in trading, then you should start by learning the basics. There are many different trading systems out there that will teach you all of these things. You can go on and learn other methods later on if you like and make sure to use them with this method for a more effective strategy. You can start by learning about some basic options strategies to gain experience using them before putting your money at risk with real trades.

Some of the most successful traders in the world combine technical analysis with fundamental analysis. The Wyckoff Method uses both these methods to try and predict future price movements.

The Wyckoff Strategy is one of the most famous methods of technical analysis around. It's also one of the simplest methods to learn because it doesn't require any complicated formulas or statistical analysis. Anyone can use this method regardless of experience level, regardless if they're an experienced investor or just starting out for the first time.

A lot of traders use books to learn the Wyckoff Method, but you should also check out webinars and videos because they'll be a lot more convenient for you.

You should always be sure that you're doing things the right way, if possible. You may want to look into some fundamental analysis or fundamental trading tools before developing any trades based on this method. This is something many successful investors do to ensure that they're not making mistakes when trading.

If you want to improve your results, then it's best if you start by incorporating this method into your strategy in some way before moving on to another one. If you like to use multiple trading strategies, then you can try developing your own strategy later on, after becoming more familiar with this method.

You may want to start out by incorporating some additional strategies into your own trading plan. It's best to start with simple strategies and then move on to more complex ones as your abilities improve. You should also try to find a system that includes a variety of different methods for diversification.

A lot of people who are new to trading often misunderstand what technical analysis is really all about, which is why they have trouble using it effectively. This is why it's important that you create an accurate definition of technical analysis. Technical analysis is the practice of using patterns, charting, and other various indicators to predict future price movements.

A lot of investors who first start out with technical analysis often misunderstand what it actually is. It's hard to know where to start if you don't have a clear idea of what technical analysis really is, which is why it's best if you learn the basics so you can get started trading effectively right away. You can find different resources to learn these techniques on your own or attend courses at local colleges and universities because they'll be a lot faster than learning everything yourself, even if you do have experience trading.

If you want to learn more about technical analysis and how it works, you can use many different resources. Many traders will start by reading books or watching videos, but if you want a quicker alternative, then courses will be a lot faster.

There are many different techniques that technical analysis is used for, but one of the most common ones is forecasting future price movements. You may hear people referring to this as charting or technical analysis forecasting, which basically comes down to using past data to predict future price movements.

Stock Selection

The first step is to select promising stocks to buy, which can be done through chart reading, technical analysis, fundamentals analysis, etc. Once a stock is selected, a trader must determine if there is any resistance area, the so-called support area, and channel lines. If it's a single stock that's being traded, then only one price channel line needs to be identified. An active stock will have multiple channels/lines to look at as it goes up and down. Once a channel line has been identified, the first Wyckoff law must be applied to determine if the channel is moving up or down based on the closing prices of the last three months' trading action.

If the channel is moving up, then the stock is considered to be in an accumulation phase. If the channel is moving down, then the stock is considered to be in a distribution phase. The next Wyckoff law will be applied to determine if it is "up" or "down" within the channel.

Support and resistance must also be identified. Support exists when there are several closes below a price level, creating a demand area for stocks, whereas resistance exists when there are several closes above a price level, creating supply in an area of stocks. The Wyckoff method teaches that support turns into resistance and vice versa by using its third law--the Law of Cause and Effect. If a stock has been in an accumulation phase and then rises above the top of the price channel, it is considered to be trading below the level of support. The Wyckoff trader will take this as a warning sign because it means that sellers are entering the market. The Law of Cause and Effect dictates that if sellers are entering the market at this time, then they must have been buying earlier to facilitate accumulation. This means that price levels at or below support will become resistant. Similarly, if an accumulation phase is coming to an end and a stock fall below support, then this area becomes support because, by definition, support goes into resistance. The Law of Cause and Effect also dictates that if buyers are leaving the market (i.e., selling) then they must have been buying earlier to facilitate accumulation. This means that price levels at or above resistance will become support.

In addition to identifying areas of support and resistance, volume can be used to assign volume profile areas for the Wyckoff investor. There are different methods of assigning volume profiles for stocks, but one method is based on the Law of Cause and Effect, which states that when demand exists, it creates volume, and when supply exists, it also creates a volume (i.e., supply creates supply). Using this method would mean that during accumulation, several periods of higher-than-average trading volume should exist; however, during distribution, fewer periods of higher-than-average trading volumes should exist.

For example, let's assume that a stock has been trading at $40 for several months and then begins a large accumulation phase. The stock is now trading at $45 or above, and the Law of Cause and Effect dictates that sellers should be entering the market. This means that there must have been buyers who were creating demand to move the price higher. As a consequence, the Law of Cause and Effect says that values below support will become resistant. In this case, once the market starts moving upward from its current level of $40, the value of the stock will begin moving upward from its current level of $45 as buyers begin to take it up from beneath its new high price level at $50. As the stock continues to rally upward, it will also begin to attract sellers who might before have not sold the stock. These sellers are now motivated to sell since they realize that their target price levels are now firmly above current levels. As the sellers take it up from beneath its current level at $60, compliance with the Law of Cause and Effect dictates that this area will become resistant because, by definition, resistance goes into support. Accordingly, as the price continues lower, it will reach an area below $40, thereby, becoming support.

The Wyckoff trader will now suggest an area of resistance around the $45 area and an area of support around the $40 level. It is important at this point to consider what would be the most logical price levels for the following reasons:

If we look at the most logical levels for this resistance and support, we find that they are at $50 and $45, respectively. Therefore, if we just remain flat with our current positions, then we may see a combination of both the resistance and support at these price levels. Because both areas are below our current price ranges, then it's possible that we might only stay flat with our positions and not move them at all. We may only move them if we see a combination of resistance and support at these price levels.

The Wyckoff method thus uses the Law of Cause and Effect as a guide, and it teaches that upward, and downward pressure can be found in prices at any level by understanding what's happening to prices at different price ranges. These movements are based on the number of sellers and buyers entering the market, which in turn is based on what types of trades are being made. As such, during accumulation, the Wyckoff trader must be alert for signals such as moving averages crossing above or below their normal ranges. During distribution, the Wyckoff trader must be alert for signals such as moving averages crossing above or below their normal ranges.

There are some problems with using the Wyckoff method. The primary problem is that every stock has its own unique history, and therefore, it is impossible to predict movements based on the same patterns. This is confusing because patterns may appear to repeat over and over again; however, stock prices can very easily move in ways that are completely different. Also, some moves made by one stock might not happen on another stock, which makes determining whether a pattern applies very confusing for traders unless they test many different stocks and patterns before making a decision.

Further, the Wyckoff method is not used by every trader. One popular Wyckoff system is based on the use of price channels (marked with double horizontal lines). Other traders use other approaches, such as seasonal charts drawn with different colors of lines instead.

Another criticism of the Wyckoff method is that it does not take into account volume. The typical trader may use a chart to determine whether or not to place a trade, but data on volume are needed to confirm that he or she has placed a bet correctly. The Wyckoff method is one of many methods of trading, and if traders are not aware of all the possibilities, it is unlikely they will be able to prepare themselves for any potential trades just because they follow a particular method.

Chapter 2: The Five-Step Approach to the Market

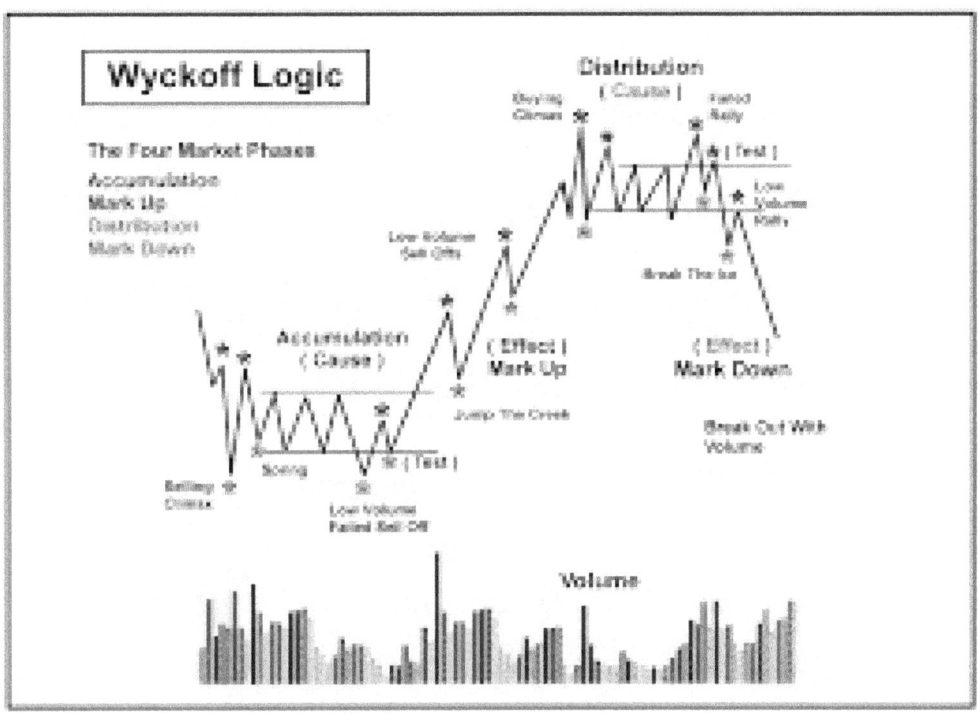

Wyckoff's method comprises five steps that help a trader to stock selection and take a position. Nevertheless, understanding all the steps is necessary to get the ultimate success.

If you want to understand Wyckoff trading price movements more deeply, check our Wyckoff Theory article

Besides, skipping one of the steps may hamper the methods. Let's jump into the Wyckoff methodology.

Step 1 – Determine the current position and possible upcoming trend of a market

It is the very first step that requires some assessment on the market. You will need to know if the market is trending in a direction or consolidating. Based on that, initiate your analysis on supply, demand, and market structure to understand the future direction of the market.

The assessment will certainly help you to decide if you need to take a long or short position in your prospective forex trading. To make your assessment more reliable, you can use point, bar, and figure charts of major forex currencies or market indices.

Step 2 – Select stocks or currencies that have synchronization with the trend

In an upward trend, it would be great if you can select the instruments that are stronger than the current market.

For example, Wyckoff suggested looking for an instrument that shows a significant percentage of the market during any tiny decreases. Alternatively, the downward trend just follows the reverse strategy and picks an instrument that is weaker than the market. However, if you are not exactly sure about the trend, it would be wise to move on to the next one.

You can also use the bar chart for the individual instruments or stocks to compare with the most relevant market data.

Step 3 – Select instrument according to the cause and effect, that also define objectives too

A critical part of Wyckoff is the trade selection and managing it through his method, which indicates the price target through the point and figures (P&F) for both short and long positions.

According to Wyckoff's cause and effect rule, the horizontal P&F count denominates the cause, while the relative price movement indicates the effect. Hence, if you aim to take a long position, select the instruments that are growing and have enough cause to satisfy your goal. The next step depends on the P&F chart of the individual instrument.

Step 4 – Select the stocks or instruments ready to rollout

Before deciding to buy or sell a forex pair, apply a nine-test rule to understand both the selling and buying test, which can be done through the supply of low-volume trading. Use a point, figure, and bar chart to identify the forex pairs.

Step 5 – Start a trade based on market dislocation

Understanding the market's fall and rise is necessary to create value while trading. So, it is helpful for the traders to buy the currencies when the market is undervalued because of the downturn and will reverse towards the upcycle.

On the other hand, individuals aiming for short positions should initiate their trade when the market has a peak. According to the Wyckoff methodology, traders should anticipate the market turn through following Wyckoff's 3-laws, which includes-

The direction of the price is determined by demand and supply.

The cause and effect relationship is responsible for market drive and prices.

The law of effort lets the traders see the price movements in advance.

Chapter 3: Wyckoff's "Composite Man"

In 1938, Charles Wyckoff published a book of his work on the "composite man." In it, he attempted to show how different charts—from astrology to the I-Ching—could be combined to create an individual human chart. Though this was not a novel idea in the history of astrology, it had never been systematically applied before.

In many ways, Wyckoff's Composite Man was revolutionary for its time because he tried to illustrate how multiple systems might be used together as one model. He hoped that by combining these systems together rather than viewing anyone as giving more credence than another, people would better understand themselves and those around them.

Wyckoff's Composite Man was intended for "students of astrology" who were already familiar with the individual systems. However, many found it difficult to read. It has been suggested that Wyckoff's intention may have been to teach astrologers how to better combine these different systems rather than provide an overly simple interpretation for lay people.

Charles E. O. Carter reflected on this book in "Wyckoff's Composite Man" (BASOR 164, 1971) by saying: "It is doubtful whether… The construction of these charts will ever become an accepted practice among astrologers. Nevertheless, I believe that Wyckoff's Composite Man has a place in the history of astrological research… They show a brilliant mind at work and may serve as models for future workers… The aim of the Composite Man is to formulate an integrated interpretation of man… Wyckoff's Composite Man contains all the elements of his method. Some may question its utility. But no one can question the soundness of its basic premise."

The "Composite Man" is a very old method of analysis for closely examining market conditions. It was pioneered by Charles Wyckoff in the 1920s and has been applied since then to analyze markets worldwide. While not all trading methods work, this one is believed to have an 80-to-90% accuracy rate, which is pretty impressive!

Wyckoff's Composite Man Method can be used on charts of any time frame up to 100 years. By analyzing the lines on the chart, traders may identify key areas where they may want to invest or protect themselves before these areas inevitably move in their favor. The method works by identifying lines of support and resistance that are very similar to current market conditions. These lines can also be compared to key points in history, which can help traders determine how far the market may move.

The Wyckoff Method uses graphology—essentially a time series chart that graphs support and resistance lines. The graph includes all the data points on the chart, including volume data, prices, open interest, etc. Lines are then drawn between pairs of data points on this graph to identify "goals" or key areas where prices will eventually find equilibrium.

One point to note about the Wyckoff Method is that it assumes the 9-to-1 Rule applies. This rule states that for every nine selling days, there will be one buying day. The composite man lines on graphology must apply this rule for them to be valid.

The Composite Man Method requires that certain points and prices on a chart be identified and agreed upon by traders before they can be reliably applied to analyze the market. These key points include:

- "Upper Turning Points" – Also called "Buy Signals," these are places where prices move above established resistance levels. Buy Signals are usually found at approximately 7-month, 18-month, 24-month, and 36-month cycles. The Wyckoff Method suggests that if prices move above the resistance level, there is likely to be a continued move upward—so trading should be exited only after the final price "turns."
- "Lower Turning Points" – Also called "Sell Signals," these are places where prices move below-established resistance levels. Sell Signals are usually found at approximately 7-month, 18-month, 24-month, and 36-month cycles. The Wyckoff Method suggests that if prices move below the resistance level, there is likely to be a continued move downward—so trading should be exited only after the final price "turns."
- "Gap Closing Points" – These are places where prices converge and often close at a new price level. These points were originally identified by Richard Wyckoff during his studies of railroad stocks.
- "Resistance" Lines – This term refers to lines drawn in blue on a chart that correspond to different levels of resistance in a stock or commodity. The lines are drawn using a variety of indicators that measure market sentiment and market conditions. These indicators include moving averages, volatility, open interest, and investor sentiment.
- "Support" Lines – This term refers to lines drawn in red on a chart that correspond to different levels of support in a stock or commodity. The lines are drawn using a variety of indicators that measure market sentiment and market conditions. These indicators include moving averages, volatility, open interest, and investor sentiment.
- "Turning Point" Lines – These are also called "Continuation" lines. This is because they connect points representing major swings in price up or down (Upper Turning Point—Lower Turning Point).

The Wyckoff Method suggests that once prices make their final "turn" (after breaking out of an Upper Turning Point) it will continue in the same direction until it reaches the next Upper Turning Point line.

The Wyckoff Method has been highly successful for traders who use it. However, traders should be aware that this method does not take long time frame price moves into account. It also does not consider secondary moves—i.e., moves made within the same trading session (e.g., retracements of an uptrend). Therefore, traders must combine the Wyckoff Method with other indicators to properly identify their trading strategies' best entries and exits.

Traders can use technical analysis to determine how far prices will go on a certain day—but these forecasts must be combined with context and market data (i.e., fundamentals) to be useful for short-term trading strategies.

- Market Capitalization – This is the market's total value of all outstanding shares traded. It can be thought of as the market's "portfolio" or "cap."
- Intraday Range – This is measured in pips or points—and it gives an investor a visual representation of the range within which prices typically fluctuate over a given time period. For example, if an investor sees that an Exchange Traded Fund tends to move between 0.10 to 0.25 points over a 15-minute time period, the Intraday Range would be 0.30 to 0.10.
- Daily Range – This is measured in pips or points—and it gives an investor a visual representation of the range within which prices typically fluctuate over a given time period. For example, if an investor sees that an Exchange Traded Fund tends to move between 0.10 to 0.25 points on any given day, the Daily Range would be 0.10 to 0.50.

Chapter 4: Three Wyckoff Laws

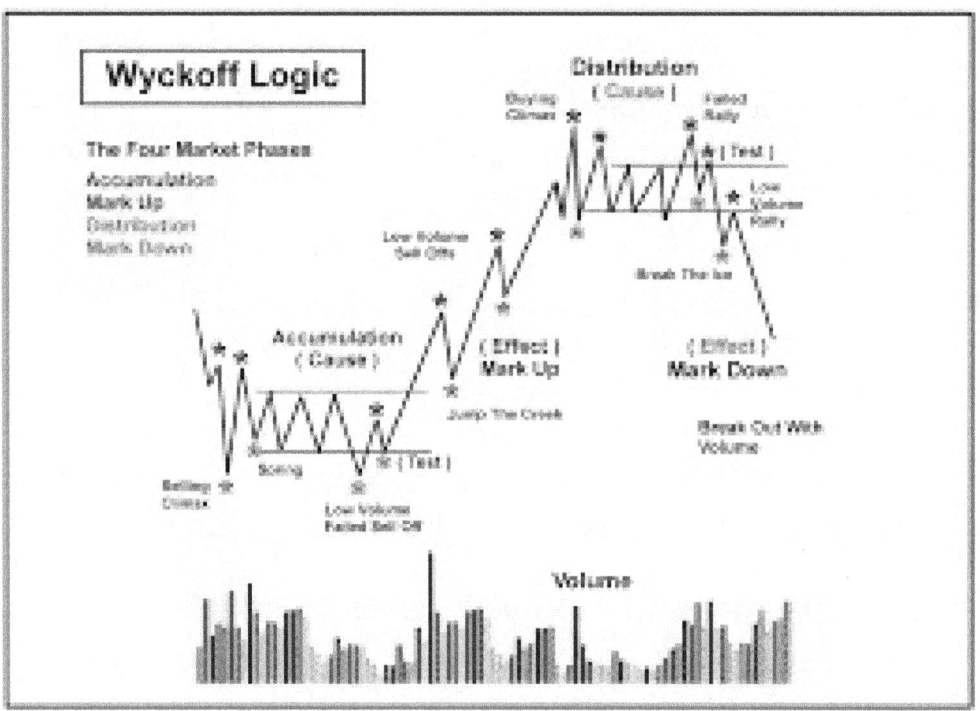

The Three Wyckoff Laws are a group of laws or rules that serve as guidelines to traders or investors in the stock market. The three laws were established by Charles P. Wyckoff, with the help of his son, who continued with him in his work, and they can be used to predict price behavior for any stock.

In today's day and age, where nearly everyone is aware of stocks but nowhere near skilled enough to make a living from them, these laws provide a valuable framework for understanding how investing works. They can also give you a sense of control over your financial future.

Wyckoff recognized the importance of the stock market as a source of wealth creation. He followed the theories of Jesse Livermore, who recognized that market-timing is possible. He also understood the importance of leverage for traders. Neither he nor his son recognized that price movements are due to psychological factors or randomness, not to any other external factor.

It is important to emphasize that these laws work only for stocks traded on major exchanges. They do not work for private company stocks or other securities, where volume is less, and there are no important exchanges where prices are published.

Wyckoff's first law is that certain parts of a stock's price movement can be predicted. In order to profit from this, you have to buy stocks near the bottom of the market and sell them near the top. You can do this by identifying these phases using Wyckoff's price and volume signals.

In the beginning, when a stock is bought, it will most likely rise within three months.

A stock starts out at $10 at Point 1, representing its lowest price in months or years. It gradually rises to $15 at Point 2, representing its highest price in months or years. After that rise, the stock returns to $10 again at Point 3, representing the low of the most recent cycle. Then it turns upward again and goes up to $20 at Point 4, representing the high of the most recent cycle.

Wyckoff's second law is that certain parts of a stock's price movement can be predicted even more easily than with his first law. Points 1 through 3 are known as accumulation phases, while point 4 is known as the distribution phase.

The basic rule concerning accumulation phases is that you should buy stocks when prices are near their lows and sell them when they are near their highs. In a stock that rises from $10 to $15, as in the example above, the first accumulation phase is from $5 to $12.50, and the second is from $12.50 to $15.

Similarly, if a stock goes down from $10 to $5, the distribution phase is from $6.00 to somewhere near its low at around a dollar or two. The first distribution phase is from around a dollar to its high at around three dollars, and the second distribution phase is from 3 dollars to 5 dollars.

Wyckoff's third law is that prices will move up or down in spurts separated by periods where they do not change much or even go slightly down. These periods are known as consolidation phases.

One way to make money is to buy stocks when they are in a consolidation phase and sell them when they are in an accumulation phase. When the stock rises, it will usually do so by around $3 or $5 at a time, and when it falls, it will usually decline by around $3 or $4 at a time. The reverse would be true for a stock that is heading downwards.

There is often the tendency to think of the stock market as some kind of casino where you risk your cash on stocks that may rise or fall with no rhyme or reason whatsoever. You can make money through the Three Laws of Wyckoff. A good software tool for helping you to implement these principles is Wyckoff Trader Plus.

The stock market has always been a complex system, but new research suggests that the nature of this complexity is changing. Traders are now able to exploit these changes, particularly in relation to the price behavior of stocks. The changes that have come about in the past decade or so are much greater than earlier thought and could well be key factors in predicting stock market performance over the next decade. As such, they suggest that investors can profit from maintaining a much greater level of surprise about their chosen stocks than earlier thought possible.

The secret to understanding the behavior of the stock market is to realize that human emotions control it. These emotions can be seen in action on any day, in any place, on the trading floor, or in the news room. They are not restricted to one side of the market or another; they are present everywhere.

There are three basic "emotions" which lead to price behavior in stocks: greed, fear, and surprise. To understand how this works, you need to be able to detect them in real time. This is where trading software comes in handy because good software enables you to predict changes in price based upon these emotions with a higher degree of accuracy than you would otherwise be able to do.

Simply being able to recognize the presence of emotion is not enough, however. A successful trader must also learn how to exploit that emotion. If that emotion is fear, you must recognize when traders are fearful of their holdings and get out of them before they realize it. On the other hand, you can take advantage of greed by being in stocks so long as the market remains greedy.

Wyckoff's work provides a template for viewing the stock market in this new light. He tracked price behavior over decades, noting every successive high and low point on stocks traded on major exchanges over time.

Chapter 5: Wyckoff Price Cycle in Depth

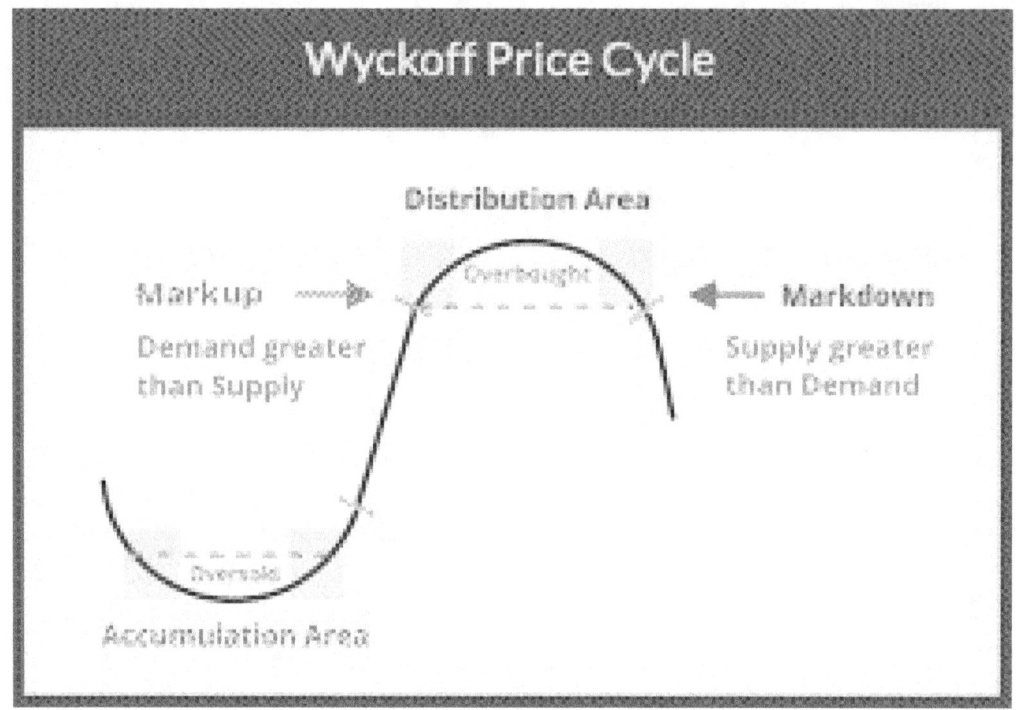

This book is intended to serve as a detailed overview of the Wyckoff Price Cycle. The Wyckoff Price Cycle has been used by traders and financial analysts for over 70 years to measure market behavior. It is often used for charting projections, acting as an indicator, predicting price movement, and identifying possible changes in the market. While there are many variations of this cycle out there, this will focus on the one that was first proposed by Benjamin Franklin in 1939, where he coined the term "Wyckoff."

The Wyckoff Price Cycle is divided into 4 stages, with each stage representing a distinct period of time. The first stage is the initial accumulation phase, the second stage is the intermediate accumulation phase, the third stage is the secondary or final accumulation phase, and finally, in the fourth stage, there will be an ultimate distribution phase.

The amplitude of this cycle varies from market to market based on many different factors. Key to this cycle is certain periods of time that appear to represent key phases for market activity. These periods are referred to as "Wyckoffs" or "Power Cycles." The traditional WPC takes place over a 5-

week cycle amplitude ranging from 1/4 wave to 3 waves in length.

The Wyckoff price cycle varies in many different ways. The way the cycles occur in different markets is crucial to the accuracy and strength of any given interpretation. There are several variations of this cycle that can be useful in different situations:

-Power Cycle: The power cycle takes place every 18 months and has an amplitude ranging from one wave to five waves. When a market is in a bull market, an intermediate accumulation phase will occur at the same time as a bear market, which is sometimes referred to as a Power Cycle or Power Wave. At the end of this intermediate accumulation phase, there will be another bull market and another bear market, which is also referred to as a Power Cycle or Power Wave. After these intermediate accumulation phases, the market enters a point in time where there is a high potential for a high percentage move in either direction.

-Primary Cycle: A primary cycle takes place every five years and has an amplitude ranging from two waves to five waves. This cycle is sometimes referred to as the Super Cycle and has been noted by Wyckoff and his followers as the most important phase of the WPC. It is known that markets, in particular stocks, can remain in this phase for many different amounts of time, up to 20 years. These periods are also known as accumulation phases and can be expected to show at least one bull market and one bear market within their own respective cycles.

-Intermediate Cycle: The intermediate cycle takes place every two to three years and has an amplitude ranging from one wave to three waves. These cycles are often referred to as the Secondary Cycle. These cycles are important phases of the WPC because they can last long periods of time, lasting anywhere from 6 months to over 5 years before entering the next phase of the WPC.

-Minor Cycle: Minor cycles take place on a monthly basis and have amplitudes ranging from one wave to three waves. Minor cycles are also called Point Waves or Minor Accumulation Waves, which occur within intermediate or primary accumulation phases.

The Wyckoff Price Cycle is an excellent tool for traders all across the world. It has proven to be accurate time after time when applied correctly. The true test of any cycle lies in its ability to be successfully traded when it is in motion. Many traders have used this cycle for decades with great success in various markets, including stocks, forex, precious metals, commodities, and options.

A very well-known trader by the name of Sheldon Natenberg wrote a book in the 1980s called the "Wyckoff Method." This book describes in detail many different aspects of the Wyckoff Price Cycle and is regarded as one of the best books concerning stock market investing ever written. He describes the following cycle that he has found to be very accurate. He has found that this cycle is very similar to the traditional figure 8 but with several differences. There are an extra pair of waves within this figure, which makes it a 10-wave cycle.

The final phase of the Wyckoff Price Cycle is an ultimate distribution phase or Lag Phase. It is during this phase where investors can take profits or cut their losses, depending on what they choose to do at this point in time. This period lasts anywhere from one to three years, depending on what stage of the WPC they are in at that time.

After the final distribution phase, the market will move on to a new accumulation phase, which is defined as being an intermediate accumulation phase. The traditional WPC cycle has an amplitude of one wave to three waves, although there are some variations that exceed this range.

Once the market has entered into this intermediate accumulation phase, it will then move into another primary or Power Cycle. This cycle typically lasts anywhere from 5 to 18 months before entering into an ultimate distribution phase. This last period of time is sometimes referred to as the Lag Phase, where investors can make their final decisions on what they want to do with their investments.

In order for traders or investors to determine if they have correctly interpreted the market movement during any phase of the WPC, they must look at a few basic indicators. Using these indicators will allow the trader or investor to see if they are on the right path. The first indicator is called "Wyckoff Price Ratios."

Wyckoff price ratios are used in conjunction with the traditional WPC cycle to determine how far away from "Quality" an investment is. A Quality is defined as a time sequence of events that establishes the market's trend. The market will move in one direction for a period of time and then turn around to move in its opposite direction for a period of time before repeating itself again. The market cannot be considered Quality if it only moves in one constant direction.

A Wyckoff price ratio is calculated by dividing any two-wave points in a wave sequence. The advantage of this calculation is that it allows the trader or investor to look at the market from a prospective that gives more detail on how far away from an important level the market may be. In other words, it will show how far away from an important level of support or resistance the market may be during any particular phase of the WPC.

There are certain indicators that will allow traders and investors to determine if they are in one of these phases during any particular cycle. The final phase of the traditional WPC is referred to as an "Ultimate Distribution Phase" or "Lag Phase."

The Wyckoff Method is a very powerful tool that many investors have used over the years. The Wyckoff method can also be applied to other markets, such as farm commodities, forex, and metals. Although this system requires a great deal of skill and experience to correctly interpret, traders and investors should consider using the Wyckoff method. The only way to become a skilled trader or investor is through education and practice. Using the learning tools provided by the market will give anyone an advantage over those who do not know what they are doing.

Chapter 6: Wyckoff Phases/Events: Accumulation and Distribution

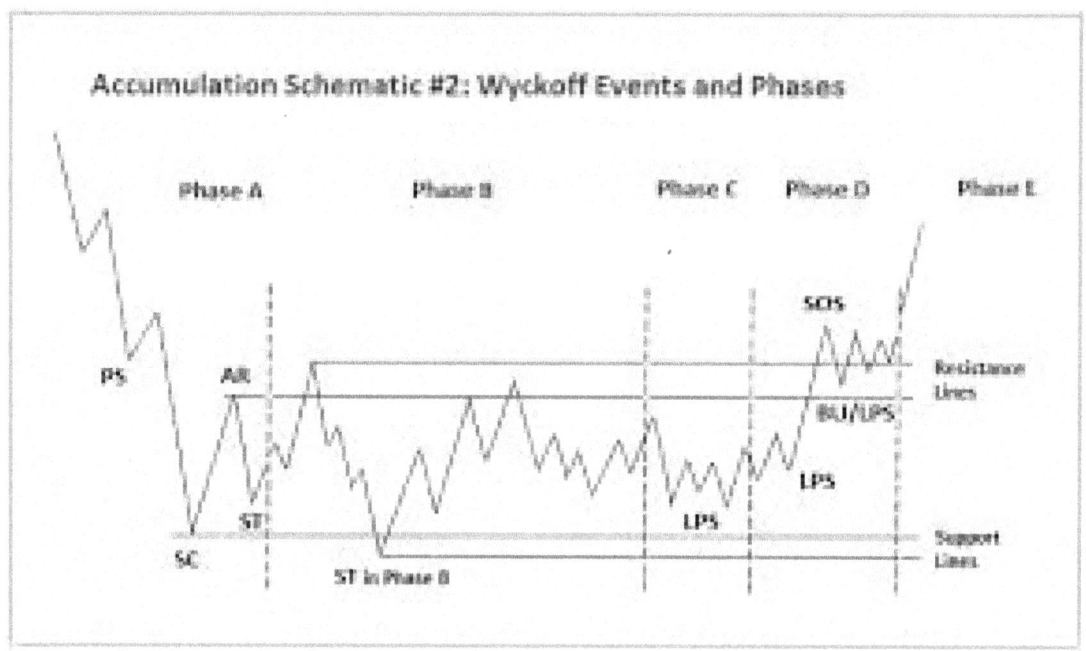

The Wyckoff Method, originally developed by Charles H. Wyckoff in the late 1800s, is an analytical method for studying stock price behavior. It breaks up the natural sequence of a bull market into four phases: accumulation, topping out, distribution, and bottom fishing.

Accumulation is marked by periods of low trading volume, while prices range between one support area and another support area that lies below it. Prices are being accumulated by investors looking to buy shares at lower prices than they were available during the prior period of accumulation or waiting for a better entry point lower down in price than they can currently find between two areas of equal resistance (a "bouncing off" effect).

This action of investors climbing into a position is also known as "crowding in." As the price approaches the lower support level, volume picks up, signaling that accumulation for this period is complete.

The second period of accumulation will be marked by declining volume as the price approaches the upper support level. This action of investors selling their position is also known as "crowding out." Once again, as the price nears the upper resistance level, the volume will pick up again. Those remaining on board at this point are expecting to exit at an even higher price than before. This often leads to a short squeeze.

Top prices are determined by the level of "crowding in." If an equal number of sellers does not match the number of new buyers entering a position, the price will continue to rise. This behavior shows that the greater the potential for profits, or "greater fool" syndrome, the more investors will buy until everyone has bought in who wants to buy at this level, creating what is known as an impasse. This impasse marks the last phase of accumulation wherein price moves upwards without hitting resistance—prices are being bought up, so little selling occurs.

Distribution is marked by periods of high trading volume while prices fall off from their highs. This action of investors selling their position is also known as "crowding out." As volume picks up, this signifies that distribution for this period is complete.

This is the fourth and final phase of the Wyckoff Method, which marks the end of a bull market. Volume typically declines as the price continues to fall.

The distribution of stock prices is divided into four phases of distribution: distribution, bottom fishing, topping out, and distribution. Distribution marks the end of a bull market; prices decline to experience subpar buying activity. Not until prices have declined through support will many investors be convinced of a permanent decline in price.

Once the last areas of distribution are complete, prices enter a period of bottom fishing, where prices will fall to their lowest point before finally turning around and entering a new bull market. During distribution, sellers dominate the marketplace, causing prices to decline. Price will fall all the way down to its lowest support level before sellers become exhausted and buyers begin accumulating shares again—the price level at which selling comes to a stop is called a demand zone.

After distribution has ended and demand zones have been formed, prices begin an initial climb back up. This initial move is known as "topping out." It signals that a completely new bull market has begun.

An impasse is a period of time where price refuses to move lower, even after a period of distribution. This can be due to strong support at preceding support levels or because new buyers entering the stock feel prices are oversold.

An impasse is an area from which an accumulation period will begin.

The accumulation period can begin at various price levels on various time duration charts. In order to make sure the start of an accumulation phase is correctly identified, one must look at both volume and price action in relation to each other and how they relate to past formations and movements in price.

According to the basic Wyckoff Cycles, there are four stages of accumulation, each with its own particular pattern of behavior. These three types of behavior coincide with the basic Wyckoff Cycles, that is:

- Accumulation Phase (Bottom Fisherman) - The accumulation phase begins when the bottom fisherman's action is reversed. This occurs in a demand zone. The bottom fisherman comes in at the price level earlier, determined by the bullish wave to have defined the bull market. The bottom fisherman buys at this price level and sells the stock immediately thereafter, causing prices to rise after he leaves.
- Accumulation Phase (Crowding In) - Once the accumulation phase is in high gear, selling can be minimized by selling into weaker demand. This is how prices are accumulated in the next area of resistance at a higher price level.
- Accumulation Phase (Crowding Out) - After prices have risen beyond the prior area of resistance, there are no more buyers left to accumulate stock at the lower price level. The number of sellers who want out is still greater than the number of buyers who want in, so the price drops back down to the support level.
- Accumulation Phase (Substitution) - After prices drop to the support level, an equal number of buyers will show up to buy the

shares at the new support level. This is how prices are accumulated in the next area of resistance at a lower price level.

After the price has risen past demand zones at higher levels in the accumulation phase, there are no longer any stock buyers in its vicinity. This results in sellers in high supply competing with each other for one chance to sell in a lower supported region. Once all these sellers have sold into this region, buyers no longer support that price level, and it will start moving back upwards towards its former demand zone. This is known as the bottom fisherman coming in at the price level earlier, determined by the bullish wave to have defined the bull market. The bottom fisherman buys at this price level and sells the stock immediately thereafter, causing prices to rise after he leaves.

As prices are being accumulated, there are always subpar buyers who are not able to purchase the stock. These people are either waiting for a better opportunity or are just not interested in buying into this particular market right now. This is because these subpar buyers see that there is more risk involved with purchasing stock at a higher price level, especially with low volume.

As prices rise, more subpar buyers begin to show interest. After the subpar buyers purchase at the new prices, they may hold on to their stock for a certain period of time. This is called "waiting for the right time" or "buying back in."

When prices drop back down to the support level after reaching new highs, no longer stock buyers are present (note that this does not mean that there are no sellers). This results in sellers in high supply competing with each other for one chance to sell in a higher supported region. Once all these sellers have sold into this region, buyers no longer support that price level, and it will start moving back downwards towards its former demand zone. This is known as the bottom fisherman coming in at the price level earlier, determined by the bullish wave to have defined the bull market. The bottom fisherman buys at this price level and sells the stock immediately thereafter, causing prices to drop after he leaves.

As prices are dropping in value, there are always various levels of support that will hold prices in place for a certain period of time before selling occurs again during a new selling opportunity. After exhibiting such signs of support, these areas (or demand zones) can be analyzed to determine when they will provide an entry point for accumulation.

Demand zones provide a good area for accumulating stock because the people who enter the area will be buying into a strong support level. At such times, prices often go nowhere but up. Conversely, rallies that breakthrough support levels without finding buyers at demand zones often do not last long and can lead to significant losses.

The accumulation period is completed when an accumulation phase ends or is prolonged. This can be due to a number of different reasons, but the most common are:

A buying count, also known as the "P count," is a term coined by Robert Prechter in his technical analysis to describe how many buyers there are in the market. The maximum number of buyers that are present at any given time regardless of their intentions, regardless of whether they are buying or selling.

The use of the word count itself has its origins back to the birth of the Stock Market itself.

Here is the stock market chart from 1817, showing what we now call a "pump and dump." The market has been in a downtrend for several years, but one of its most common patterns was a bounce upwards during the nineteenth century. A buying spree began, and the market rose to the point where it broke through several significant levels of support. This kind of rally is referred to as a "P&D."

Note how it is very rare for stocks to break through support without some kind of buying counting accompanying it. In this case, there were three phases, with an accumulation phase occurring on each occasion as well as a new demand zone being established on each occasion.

These buying counts can be used to determine if accumulation has occurred. If the price is approaching a support level, but no buyers present near that support, then there may be an accumulation period. These points are labeled.

Buying counts can also be used to determine when prices have reached the maximum number of buyers in the market. The advantage of using P&D patterns for this is their reliability and accuracy when compared to other methods.

The significant demand zones are highlighted by the vertical lines at points A, B, C, D, E and F on this chart. The formula used to establish these points is as follows:

Starting at the demand zone (D), move vertically upwards until you reach the highest price that was paid during the accumulation phase (E). Then, extend that level (E) to the right by 50% of its value.

To determine where a new bull market will begin, take your starting price (A) and move horizontally to the left by 50% of its value. This point will be your new starting point for a new bullish wave. By using these significant demand zones as an area for future accumulation, one can construct a very reliable model for future trends.

Demand zones can be used to generate buy signals for future accumulation. The formula for this is as follows:

Take the price of the stock at its current level (A). Move vertically upwards until you reach the highest price that was paid during the accumulation phase (B). This will give you your 50% retracement of B. To determine where your buy signal will occur, move horizontally to the left by 50% of B and draw a vertical line on your chart marking this point. Then, move horizontally to the right by an amount equal to 0.735 times B and draw a horizontal line on your chart marking this point as well as a sell signal or resistance level.

Buying signals can also be used to determine when prices will fall. To do this, simply take the 50% retracement of B and draw a vertical line downward, starting at that point marked by the highest price paid during the accumulation phase (E). Then, move horizontally to the right by an amount equal to 0.735 times B and draw a horizontal line on your chart marking this point as well as a sell signal or support level.

The support level is the least resistant point in an accumulation period, where price often stalls when it is unable to move lower. It can be used to establish an important buying zone when price approaches so that when price does break through, it will provide strong buying pressure to propel the stock higher. As prices develop more strength, they will continue moving towards more resilient levels of support until they are exhausted. Once this happens, the result is usually a breakdown of the trend.

The resistance level is not a price or an actual level, but rather a point at which there is a significant amount of resistance against the stock. This resistance can come from a number of factors, but it will be strong enough to prevent the trend from moving higher. If one's trend following indicator hits this resistance level, then they should expect the stock to move lower rather than higher. Resistance levels can often be found just below significant peaks in price, where stock often begins to stall and reverse its direction as the bulls retreat from their efforts to climb any further.

Support/resistance levels are very important for trend followers to use, as they are the strongest point against which they can gauge how strong an accumulation phase has become. A stock reaching a resistance level may be considered an interruption of the trend, meaning that some kind of accumulation phase will occur to restore the trend. If one's support/resistance levels are inaccurate or out of date, then this may cause one to miss signals or accumulate too early or too late.

Support points are important to bear in mind when stock is close to a significant support level. Often, there is a strong buildup on either side of this level before actual support turns up. If one can detect these patterns of accumulation, then one can use them to provide more accurate future estimates of support levels.

Retracements are periods of price movement during which price trends seem to be slowing down or stalling. They are an indication of the strength, or lack thereof, of the current trend. A retracement happens when a stock reaches resistance and reverses its direction for a short period of time before continuing in the same direction it was earlier trending in. Retracements can be thought of as counter-trend moves that occur after a trend has generated enough momentum to reach an obstacle that appears to be too strong for it at that point in time.

Retracements are important to bear in mind when approaching support levels. Often, there is a strong buildup on either side of this level before actual support turns up. If one can detect these patterns of accumulation, then one can use them to provide more accurate future estimates of support levels.

The characteristics that form during accumulation are present in many types of markets, both sideways, and trending, but are most noticeable in the sideways markets. Accumulation periods may last for months or even years at a time, but they provide great opportunities to generate profits with high accuracy when properly analyzed.

The important factor with the accumulation techniques is that they were designed for use by trend followers rather than long-term investors. They should not be used if the intention is to keep the stock for long-term gain. Market reversals are a common part of day-to-day price movements, whether you are an expert or just starting out. Only experienced traders should try to predict price direction.

If there are more than 3 consecutive up days within a month, then it is best to expect a trend reversal to occur soon. If there are only 2 consecutive down days within a month, then consider holding on until the third day before selling. If you decide to sell based on this technique, take profits at your next stop loss level instead of selling at exactly 1% below your entry point.

Be careful when using technical indicators. They can provide you with confirmation of a signal but do not rely on them to make your buy/sell decisions for you. Read what analysts and economists are saying about the company, and try to determine why the price is going up or down before buying or selling the stock.

Small Orders

The opposite of accumulating a position is distributing it. The method for distributing a position is opposite that of accumulation:

- If the trader bought at A, then sell at B where B = (1-(A/B) x 100) x (P)0.735 + 0.1 = B.
- If the trader bought at B, then sell at A where A = (1-(B/A) x 100) x (P)0.735 + 0.1 = C

The larger the difference between the entry and exit prices, the stronger the signal to buy or sell is considered.

Spread Betting

Spread bets are bets on two or more stocks that any single brokerage firm does not cover. Unlike covered options, which require multiple trades to be executed, spread bets can be placed in one transaction using just one contract size. Spread bets give the trader the opportunity to receive a yield in addition to capital gains. All spread bets are placed using the margin system.

Spread betting for profits differs from playing stocks in that it is not based on analyzing price movements, but rather on predicting price movements. The trader sets a risk level and then sets up multiple options (the 'bets') at his chosen risk level. The market either confirms the trader's prediction or does not; if it does, he profits and can re-open new positions accordingly, provided he has enough money in his account to open new positions at the same risk level he closed at when the last trading. If the market does not confirm his prediction, then he loses his bet.

Spread bets can be set on any asset value (such as the stock price, currency exchange rates, commodities), and traders can choose their own risk levels. A trader is, therefore, free to choose any level of risk that they feel comfortable with while still having the opportunity to win a profit. They do this by buying or selling spreads at a calculated percentage above or below a certain level in order to earn a profit if the price of the asset moves in a certain direction.

The trader can also play spread bets using other spread betting companies other than his own account provider. For example, traders can set up a spread bet with another online broker to play against their own investment decisions. This is known as switching and is an effective tool for the experienced trader as it allows them to generate capital gains (or reduce losses) whenever they want.

Spread betting can be a useful tool for those who like to trade large amounts because it allows the trader to play numerous scenarios at once, placing multiple bets against each other. It can be especially useful for those who like to gamble and choose many different options and then exit trades (or profit from them) as they see fit. It is not a good idea to trade large amounts with a single bet if you do not have a significant amount of money in the account.

While spreads bets are a useful tool for advanced traders, it is not recommended that new or inexperienced traders use them since they may do more harm than good. Spread betting can be extremely dangerous for individuals who embark on the path of technical trading without really understanding what this means. These individuals often fall prey to possible emotions such as greed and fear and neglect education on how to make effective stock selections. Experienced traders often lose because they are not able to keep their emotions in check after doing well for a period of time.

Moving Averages

Moving averages are indicators that can be set to eliminate chart jitters, noise, and distortions created by the rising and falling prices during the day. They are based on mathematical calculations that average out all price movements. Traders use them as a guide to decide whether prices are stable or fluctuating, and they help determine trends rather than market directions. Moving averages help to identify the trend.

Most moving averages are plotted on a chart. They show simple mathematical calculations of how many days the closing price is above its opening price compared to the average number of days it stays above its opening price. If the price is below its moving average, then it is said to be in a downtrend. A rising line with no time period defines an uptrend. It shows that prices are higher than their average above the normal level and begins to regress after a while, which means they return back to their moving average.

Moving averages can take various forms, such as simple exponential, lagging, and leading moving averages. Simple exponential moving averages (SEMA) are the most common type of moving average. It is calculated by adding the sum of all prices for a specific period and dividing by the number of days.

SEMA is considered to be lagging because its signals are two days behind the current price action. A simple exponential moving average with a five-day value will be used as an example to explain this concept further. If today's closing price is $32, then SEMA will be $25 (five-day average), $28 (four-day average), $30 (three-day average) $31 (two-day average), and $32 (today's closing price).

The TOC is in a different font

A lagging moving average will always be behind the current price movements. It is the opposite of a leading moving average that will be ahead of the price.

A simple exponential moving average with a five-day value will be used as an example to explain this concept further. If today's closing price is $32, then SEMA will be $25 (five-day average), $28 (four-day average), $30 (three-day average) $31 (two-day average), and $32 (today's closing price).

If the price drops below its moving average, it is said to be in a downtrend. A rising line with no time period defines an uptrend. It shows that prices are higher than their average above the normal level and begins to regress after a while, which means they return back to their moving average.

The first thing you should know about using moving averages is that it should not take the place of fundamental analysis, technical analysis, or other strategies. It can be used in conjunction with them to help improve the accuracy of your predictions.

Short-term moving averages can be used like stop-losses when you believe there is a trend in the market. It will help you decide when to enter or exit trades. Focus on the fast line when placing stop-loss or take-profit orders. If the price is above its moving average, then it can provide a more accurate level for your entry into the market.

Price goes below its EMA then it will usually move back up to it, but not always. If you place a buy order above the EMA, then your goal is to sell when the price goes above this moving average for an increase in profit. The same is true for selling when the price drops below its EMA. It will probably regain the earlier levels and eventually move back to the earlier price level after a breakout.

Moving averages do not always provide accurate signals as they should, but using them in conjunction with other strategies such as fundamental analysis and technical analysis can help you become a better trader.

Stop-Loss Systems

A stop-loss system is one of the most effective strategies that can be used to minimize risk in trading. It is a way of limiting the amount of loss you will take on a trade, even if it has large profit potential.

When you set stop-loss orders, you are letting the market know that you will be exiting your trade in the event that the price moves against you. If you do not take action, then your loss can grow much larger than if you were to take action.

Let's assume that when the stock price rises by 5% today in one day, it will probably drop back in value in a few days, but in 2 weeks, it will probably rise again in price. By entering a stop-loss order at 5% (below its moving average) when buying would be like saying, "Buy me, but if this stock goes down by more than 5% within 1 day, then get out of this trade. If it does not go back up or does not move for more than 1 or 2 days, then sell me."

If the stock moves down to 3%, you will be happy because you are out of this position, but if it goes back up to 5%, you will probably take another loss of 5%. If the stock later moves back down to 2%, the first thing you should do is sell it because it is likely lower than its moving average. You would be glad that you were out of the trade so early on. At some point, if the price keeps going against your stop-loss order, then you should place a new stop-loss order at 10% below your last purchase price that was above its moving average. This will be your new stop-loss order.

If you keep placing these stop-loss orders every time the stock moves up, then, eventually, it will limit the amount of money you can lose on a trade.

Technical Analysis

Technical analysis is used to predict the direction of a stock by using historical price data and using that information to predict future price movements. A common way of doing technical analysis involves studying past prices, charts, and patterns in order to find favorable trading opportunities.

One of the most important things to understand about technical analysis is that it is just one of many strategies that can be used for trading. Technical analysis does not always provide you with the best price predictions, but it can provide very accurate future price movements if used in conjunction with other methods, such as fundamental analysis.

One simple way to use technical analysis is to study charts and find patterns that frequently appear in the market. The more time a pattern repeats itself, then you can use that pattern in a prediction or a trade.

The most commonly used technical indicators are moving averages, Bollinger Bands, and the MACD. Moving averages is one of the most important technical indicators that you can use in conjunction with other techniques. It is an indicator that represents the average price of a stock over a specific period of time, such as 10 days or 20 days. It can be used to determine short-term and long-term trends in a stock and to identify the strength or weakness of a trend.

Bollinger Bands is another indicator that can be used to help determine future prices. It measures volatility by using price bands above and below its moving average; the upper band represents resistance and will act as a barrier to further gain. The lower band represents support and will act as a barrier to further loss.

The MACD is similar to the moving averages, but it uses the difference between the two moving averages in order to measure volatility. It can be used in conjunction with Bollinger bands in order to determine whether an uptrend is about to end.

You will learn more about each of these technical indicators when you are creating your own trading system that uses them in combination with other tools such as fundamental analysis.

Fundamental Analysis

When you are looking at the price charts of any company, you are looking at their financial statements. Companies do not have a financial statement because they are trying to deceive you. They have a financial statement because they want to be as open and transparent as possible.

If you do your homework and look at the company's financial statements, then you will know whether or not to enter into a trade with that company. The first thing that you should check is the gross profit margin which should be greater than 40%.

The second thing that you should look at is the debt-to-equity ratio, which shows how much debt a company has compared to its stockholders' equity. The debt-to-equity ratio should be less than 30% or even 10%.

The third thing you should look at is the return on equity, which shows how much profit has been generated by the company's shareholders. It should be greater than 10%.

The fourth thing that you should look at is revenue growth because it shows how well a company is growing its business. If there is no revenue growth, then it means that there is no potential growth in the future. There are many times when stocks are purchased because of their recent huge gains but do not have any real underlying value.

When you are looking at a stock for investment purposes, you must be aware of all of its fundamentals, not just whether or not it will go up in value based on historical price movements. If there is no growth in the company, then there is no growth in its stock.

If you compare the price of any stock to another similar company, you should be looking at the current ratio. The current ratio tells you how much the company has available to pay out to its shareholders. If a company has a lot of cash that it can payout, then that means that it has many customers and customers are willing to buy their products because they are getting good value for their money. If companies have lots of customers, then they will buy more products because they do not want to lose them to other companies, so they will be willing to pay higher prices for products or services.

The current ratio should be greater than 3.0. If the company is less than 3.0, then it means that they are missing out on making profits by not paying out more money to their shareholders. If you think about it, this would make sense because companies do not want all their money paid out to shareholders for them to go out and spend it on unnecessary things instead of investing in the business, which would help increase sales and profits in the long run.

You must also look at the debt-to-equity ratio in order to know how much debt is outstanding in a company. The debt-to-equity ratio should not be more than 30%.

The last thing that you should look at is the cash flow. You can get a better feel for the company's management by looking at their free cash flow. This is what you make when you do not take out any debt, and there is no capital expenditure. Free cash flow should be greater than net income and lesser than operating income.

You can compare current free cash flow with historical free cash flow to determine whether or not the stock has had steady growth over time. This would mean that there was some depth in the company's value, and there is potential for new growth in the future.

Consistent Price Movement

Consistent price movement in a stock is something that you should monitor when you are trading stocks. There are many ways that you can monitor this. You can check the charts in order to see how often it repeats its movement over time. If there are no rapid movements up or down in the stock, then this means that there is no real growth in the company, and if there is no growth in the company, then there will be no growth in the stock price.

You can also look at how much it fluctuates when compared to another similar company and whether or not one of them has greater fluctuations than the other. If one of them has greater volatility, then it means that there is something going on in the company which you will want to research further.

A stock must always have consistent price movement for you to be able to profit. If it does not, then this is an indicator that the system behind the price action is broken, and there is no way for you to profit.

Reversal Points

When looking at charts, you will notice what are known as reversal points. These are pointing that act as resistance or support when prices are moving up or down, respectively. You can calculate these reversal points very easily by just taking the 52-week high or low and subtracting it from the current price of a stock. This gives you the point of resistance and support and also tells you when to get ready to sell or buy a stock. For example, if the current price is $10 and the 52-week high is $13, then the reversal point is +$3. If you want to find out when it will be a good time to get in or out of a trade with that particular stock, then you would add the price difference from the reversal point with three months' time for protection for your trade. If there are more than six months until the next reversal point, then this would mean that there was a significant risk in going short or long because there is a great possibility for profit or loss if the price makes a new low/high in that timeframe.

Insider Trading

Insider trading can be very beneficial to investors. It is when an individual takes advantage of non-public information that is currently well known throughout the market in order to profit. For example, if you are at a company that makes products for mining companies and you know that your company is well on its way to making a new discovery in their mine, then it would be considered insider trading if you do not buy or sell your stocks before this important news breaks when it will likely send the stock price flying in one direction.

Insider trading can be very risky, and you should do your research before you decide to engage in this practice. There are times when an insider buys a large block of shares knowing that their company is about to go bankrupt and then takes all the money and runs, leaving thousands of other shareholders with worthless stocks. There are also times when insiders will take all of their money and quit working at their job in order to avoid paying taxes on it, or they will buy up as many stocks as they can as soon as the price starts moving higher.

The last thing that you should remember about insider trading is that it is illegal for those who do not have enough information about the company to trade on this type of information. If you are in a company, then it is your job to make sure that everything is running smoothly, and you need to keep up with all the information in order to make wise decisions in regard to the company. If you do not, then you could lose a lot of money when it comes time to sell your stock.

Chapter 7: How Markets Move

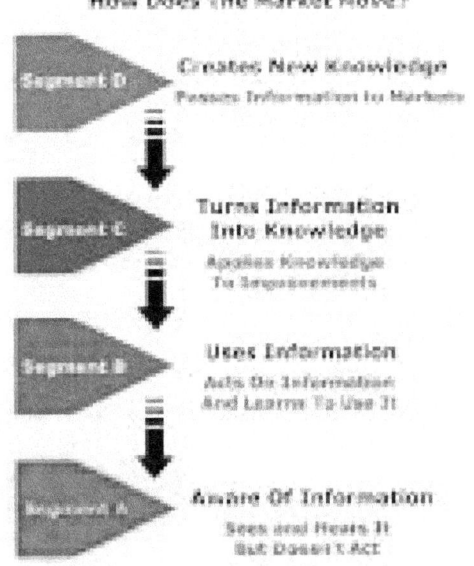

The stock market is a continuous moving average, composed of a series of up and down trends each day. The effect of the market rises and falls over a period called "the trading day." When it opens, values are at their highest for two hours until they fall to the lowest point at the closing bell. Investors buy a stock when its value is highest or sell it when it has fallen too low. In doing so, they believe that they could gain more money by buying low and selling high than if they just remained invested in stocks. The volatility of markets also makes investing difficult because you never know what will happen from one minute to the next.

The stock market process is natural. It is based on supply and demand. Because of the large amount of money involved, however, it has become very political. Interest groups seek to use the market to serve their own purposes. Stock market investors base their decisions on price chart patterns, technical analysis indicators, and fundamentals. They use these tools to predict the outcome of their investment decisions with some level of confidence.

Through this, you will learn how markets move and how you can apply this information to your investments.

How Markets Move: A Historical Perspective

Since its early days, investors have used different methods to predict the outcome of investing in stocks based on their position on the stock value graph. In the 1920s, investors bought stocks when they started trending upward and sold them when they went downward. At that time, stock prices were not continuous from one trading day to the next. In the 1930s, a man named George Lane formulated a system called "trend-following analysis," which uses past performance patterns to make its decision.

In the 1960s, Edgar Peters improved these techniques by using charts of historical stock price movements to ensure his analysis was accurate. In 1965 he published a book called How Markets Move, which became a classic in the investment world. Its success led to other books that used trend-following analysis methods.

How to Use the Method?

If you are interested in investing in stocks, you can use trend-following analysis to decide if it is a good time to invest in the stock market. To do so, take a chart of any stock you are interested in buying and find out how it has moved historically. Then, look at the following four questions:

Is the current price above or below its historical trend? If above, then there is an upward trend. If below, then there is a downward trend. Is this stock currently trending? If yes, then it has a bullish trend. If no, then it has an overall bearish trend (i.e., downtrend). Has the stock continuously trended in the same direction over time? If yes, then you can expect it to continue trending in this direction. But if you've seen a pullback in value in this area before, then the trend has changed. Has the stock trended in the same direction for at least one year? If yes, then it has a very strong uptrend. If not, then it is more likely that you will see a downtrend.

Once you have answered these questions for each of the stocks you are interested in investing in, decide if it is a good time to invest based on your analysis. If the answer is yes, then buy!

The Problem with Trend Following

The biggest problem with the trend-following analysis is that it does not tell you when to stop buying your stock. You can be wrong in your analysis and sell at the wrong time. If you do so, there will be a loss. If you are wrong, you can lose more than just the price of your stock because you will have wasted money on commissions to your broker for selling shares. So, it is important to get this right before investing in any stocks.

Trend-Following Analysis Will Help You Win More Money! Written by professional trader Ozzie Slone, this book contains everything that every investor wants to know about how markets really work. One of the great benefits of buying this book is that Slone makes his own investments.

In addition, if you are going to buy a stock, you should wait for a pullback in the stock before investing in it. A pullback occurs when a stock has risen above its prior high or fallen below its prior low, with little movement between these two points. When so many investors are buying a stock that it has reached a strong resistance against any further increase or fall, it is probably time to buy. In this case, your analysis will be correct, and you will win big once the price falls back down to where you bought your shares.

However, if you are wrong in your analysis, the fall could be toward even lower levels. If that happens, you will lose all the money that you have spent on commissions to your broker. You may also lose more money because the stock drops below its prior low. This type of price drop is called a "panic sell-off," and there are no guarantees that it will go down to zero. If this happens, you will be buying at the bottom of a major bear market or recession. You may not be able to recover any of your money for years because there are no buyers during these depressing times.

In addition, the conventional trend-following analysis does not tell you when to sell a stock. You may buy a stock, and it will rise upward in value until it hits a level of strong resistance against any further increase. In this case, the price will continue going up until you make a decision to sell. Since you have been right in your analysis, you should feel confident that the stock price will rise beyond what you bought for and may even double or triple the amount of money that you originally spent on your shares! However, if that happens, it is time to sell because there may be an even bigger upward movement in the stock price above these resistance levels before you can sell at a profit. If you keep your shares too long, you could lose all your money from buying the stock in the first place. You may also see a downswing that will cause you to lose even more money.

In this case, the conventional trend-following analysis does not tell you when to sell a stock and when to buy it. If anything, it will tell you when to stop buying or selling, but it is up to you (the investor) to decide when and how much of your money should go in and come out of any investment. This methodology can be very risky because the conventional trend-following analysis is based on past history rather than future events. In other words, it is based on data from earlier decades and does not consider all possible future events.

If you buy and sell based on conventional trend-following analysis, then you will win big only if your analysis is correct. If your analysis is wrong, then you can lose money faster than a rocket ship leaving earth! This type of investing can be very stressful because you do not know when or what to buy or sell. You may also lose all your money just because the market does not move in the direction that you need to make a profit.

What About Trend-Following Trading?

A trend-following trading plan considers current trends along with past trends in order to make good trading decisions. It is not based solely on past data, but also considers possible future data. This type of investing is much harder to understand because you are not simply deciding where to buy or sell your stocks based on your analysis. You are also buying and selling based on current trends along with all possible future events.

With trend-following trading, you are looking for trades that will be profitable in the long term and in the short term. This means that you must be able to do a detailed market analysis for every stock that you follow and determine if it will make a profitable trade. If it does not make a profit in the short term, then it may become a longer-term trade after several price swings upward or downward in price. As the stock price moves in the desired direction, it may become a short-term trade that allows you to take profits in the short term without losing money.

Is this easy? No, it is not easy to do this kind of analysis because you are also keeping an eye open for any possible adverse effect on your investment. If anything occurs that could cause a stock price to drop or rise quickly then you must analyze these events and decide if your investment should remain as a long-term investment or be sold at a profit before losses occur. In addition, you must consider any favorable events that could occur that will cause the stock price to rise even more. This includes both current and future events.

In addition to considering whether a trade will make a profit or loss, you must also consider the "size" of your investment as well as your investment time frame. If you invest too much money in an investment before it makes a profit, then you will not be able to take any profits because the stock price has dropped and/or you will lose all your money if the stock price reaches its prior low.

In addition, if you invest too much money into an investment that is taking too long to produce a profit, then you can lose all your initial investment and even more than what you originally spent because the stock price has dropped and/or it has reached its prior low. Once the price drops below where you bought your shares, then it will be very difficult to get back to your cost's basis. This can cause you to lose more money than if you simply sold the stock prior to the price drop.

Finally, how much time do you have? If you buy a stock or other commodity that goes down in price, then there is no time limit on when you should sell it back. However, if you are right about an investment but do not act within the time frame to take profits, then other investors may buy this investment even cheaper than what you bought it for. In other words, if you bought a stock at $20 and waited too long to sell it back for a profit, then the stock price may rise to $30. If you decide to sell it back at $30, then you may get $28 or less because other investors were waiting for your sale, and they will buy the stock even cheaper!

If you make a bad decision and pay too much money for an investment, then you can lose all your money doing this type of investing. If you are too slow to realize that you are losing money, then the investment will quickly become a disaster. Even if you are right, but do not act within the time frame to sell back for a profit, then you will lose money by doing this type of investing. If you try to hold on to an investment that is falling in price and acting like a loser, then your investment becomes a loser, and there is no way to get your losses back.

However, if you buy an investment at the right time and do not lose any money from it falling in price, then trend-following trading will make you richer than most people. In fact, if you do the right type of investing with good timing, then many people will think that you are a genius. But it is not easy to become a trend-following trader because you must be able to determine when an investment will become a winner and when it can become a loser. Even if you are great at this kind of analysis, you must also be able to determine when an investment will make a profit and when it can make a loss.

In order to become a trend-following trader, then your biggest challenge is to decide which investments will become winners in both the short term and in the long term. You must also be able to determine when a stock will become a loser in the short term and when it will become a winner in the long term. In addition, you must be able to determine when an investment will make a profit and when it can make a loss. You must also sell any investment that is going down in price before it goes too far down in price. However, if your prediction is wrong, you may lose all your money quickly if the stock goes up too quickly!

There are many people who try to do this type of investing on their own because they think they can do this better than professionals. However, they only do this because they think they are good at it. Most people are not great at any kind of analysis or foresight to make these kinds of predictions.

Trend following is one of the most demanding risk management styles of investing because you must monitor your investments every day and determine when an investment will make a profit or loss in either the short or long term. If you are wrong, then you will lose money quickly because many of these investments can become losers overnight. When you become a trend-following trader, you must be able to make accurate predictions about the stock market's short-term and long-term price trends.

Trend following is one of the most difficult trading styles to master because there are many factors that come into play when making predictions about how investments will perform in either the short or long term. This means that it is quite possible for an investment to go up or down very quickly and that it is highly probable that there will be losses in this type of trading. However, it can be profitable and can also help you learn about your investing abilities and how the markets work.

However, there are many trend-following traders who will not follow their strategies once they begin to lose money. They simply become too afraid to follow their trend-following strategies, and this is because they did not think about how much money they could lose in a short amount of time! If you get into this type of trading where you get on losing streaks, then you will literally be trying to get out of the market before losing more money. This strategy will never work for most investors because they need the market to recover quickly and turn around in order to make a profit. They also have to have the patience to wait for the market to turn back in their favor.

If you want to become a trend-following trader, then your best strategy is to put all your money into one type of investment and not get distracted by other things. This will help you get focused on making money and following trends so that you can be sure that you will make a profit. However, if you do not take this approach, then it may be quite difficult to follow trends or even know whether an investment is going up or down in price. Since most trend-following strategies are based on short-term price changes, you need to be able to analyze them to get the best results.

This is where you will have to work harder than most other people because there is so much involved with these types of investments. For example, if you want to track where a stock will be in the present and how it will perform over the next few months or years, then it means that you must start looking for trends and making predictions before buying or selling any stocks. If you do not follow trends and patterns well enough, then it may be quite difficult for your investment to win. However, if you do follow the trends well enough, then you will be able to predict where a stock will go before making a profit or loss.

It is quite important to look for patterns and make predictions about whether an investment is going up or going down in price in the short term and long term. However, this can be difficult because many people will find that they cannot make accurate predictions about how any investment will perform over a long period of time. This is the main reason why most trend-followers only follow short-term trends because it is much easier to predict what will happen to a stock in the next few weeks or months.

However, this does not mean that it will be easy because there are many different factors that come into play when you start making predictions. Many people will try to get rid of these factors by relying on a trend-following system, and they think that if they follow a certain system, then it will be easy for them to make predictions. However, there are many things that can come into play when trying to figure out whether an investment will go up or down in price.

When it comes to buying and selling stocks, there are many different things that can affect the price of a stock. For example, if a company is not doing well, it may use public relations (PR) to get rid of negative information. This will make investors want to buy the stock and cause the price to go up because they think they can make a profit by buying shares while others do not know about the bad news. However, if you keep track of how this company performs and look at all the negative information periodically, then you may be able to predict when the stock might go up or down in price.

There are many different factors that come into play when you are trying to figure out whether an investment will go up or down in price. For example, if you think that a company is going to go bankrupt or cannot pay its debts, you might be able to predict the stock price before it happens. If this happens, then you can buy shares before they go up in price and sell them after they have come down. There are many different reasons why certain stocks will go up or down in price, and most people do not think about these things because they rely on their investments for income instead of looking ahead at how much money they can make over the next few months.

The following is one of the most difficult types of trading because you will need to know when certain stocks are going to make profits or losses. If you do not start this strategy when you are young, then it may be quite difficult for you to follow trends until you get older. This means that most trend-following traders begin their trading in their late teenage years and start their investing careers in their early twenties. However, there are many traders who will not begin their trend-following strategies until they are in their thirties because they want to become more experienced before starting out with these trades.

This trading strategy is very difficult because you will need to follow trends and patterns without getting too distracted by other things. Since most trend-following traders will be focusing on price changes in the next few weeks or months, you will need to look for patterns quickly so that you can come up with predictions about where a stock will go. If you cannot do this, then it may be quite difficult for you to trade stocks because it could take weeks or months before an investment starts to move into its growth period.

If you want to become a trend-following trader, it is important that you look at many different investments and figure out which ones could give the greatest profits over the next year or two. For example, if you study many different stocks over the next few months and find that the price is going up, then you may want to buy these stocks. If you see that a stock will go down in price quickly or make money in the short term, then you may want to sell your shares before they go down in price. However, there are many different types of investments, and this can make it very difficult for most people who are trying to follow trends because they do not know which ones could be profitable or which ones will end up losing money.

Many people like to use trend-following strategies because it is much easier than trying to predict what will happen with an investment over a long period of time. However, if you want to become a trend-following trader, then you will need to study many different investments and figure out which ones could be profitable or lose money in the coming months or years. If you do not look at many different investments and try to find patterns quickly, it may be quite difficult for you to follow trends until you get older.

Chapter 8: Can Retail Traders Actually Move the Market?

Nowadays, retail traders are the ones that feed the quantitative trading machines of Wall Street. These individuals aren't just playing around in their spare time on some penny stocks' website with $1 trades.

Their actions can literally create changes in the Stock Market that can affect worldwide working-class people in every country on Earth with the single click of a button.

It is a fact that retail traders are playing a growing role in the Stock Market, and the result of this has been larger swings in prices. In May 2010, retail stocks had a large effect on major S&P 500 price movements that rose or fell from 3% to 6%. This seems like a lot, but it's not so bad compared to stock market moves in 1987 and 2008.

The recent jump in volatility has shifted more trades towards the institutional side and away from individual investors. But is this shift in equity trading towards institutional investors affecting US Stock Market activity?

According to Fed researchers, US stock price moves are only 0.08%

correlated with the level of Treasury bond yield fluctuations. This is not much considering that equity investments are based on future income streams from firms, which depend on future interest rates. Bond prices directly affect interest rates, which can be seen in long-term charts of the bond market and its correlation with the S&P 500 Index. Equity markets are directly affected by interest rate changes in bond markets because small companies rely heavily on bond markets to finance their growth, but large firms can do fine without bonds because they have access to capital markets directly through equity offerings. The problem is that the stock market has become increasingly efficient, and now traders are not so dependent on such macro-economic factors, such as interest rates.

Today's markets are driven by information rather than economic fundamentals and news flow. A look at today's financial media shows that there is a lot of focus on the Fed stimulating the economy with quantitative easing, following up on their preceding statement that future QE purchases will remain at $85 billion per month. There will be more news about this in 2013, as it is likely to happen again next year. We also know that the inflation rate has been dropping rapidly since 2011 and will probably continue to do so with oil prices staying low and supply growing (thanks to fracking). The Fed may feel that they are doing all that they can do with the Asset Purchase Program, but investors will remain on edge until there is clarity on future US monetary policy.

The retail traders are not of the same opinion of Fed's QE program either. They don't want more QE bond purchases because it would mean higher bond prices. The retail traders are also not in support of the new Fed Chair Janet Yellen, who is expected to continue with bond purchases at the current pace. According to reports, there is growing criticism over QE3 from global equity markets, but this hasn't had much effect on US stock markets yet. The markets are still very optimistic about the economic recovery, and if they continue to be, then we might see a strong rally in the S&P 500 Index in the second half of 2013.

It seems that there is a lot more to trading than just looking at charts, following trends, and being quick on the buy/sell button. It is also more difficult than just throwing some money at your favorite stock and expecting it to grow, even though there is no visible support or resistance of value at the moment. Trading has become a lot more of a high-contact sport, with retail traders putting their money where their mouth is. Have they become too risky?

It's not like the retail traders are actually moving the market. They are just getting more bearish on equities before the Fed does. If they manage to predict the market's direction, then there might be spikes in volatility that could lead to unexpected opportunities. Just because one person can move markets doesn't mean that it's not possible for retail traders to move them again, especially if their moves affect large portions of shares in a Stock Market Index.

The bottom line is that retail traders will continue to play a very important role in the Stock Market, and don't be surprised if small moves matter for many investors this year and next.

Chapter 9: Supply and Demand Analysis

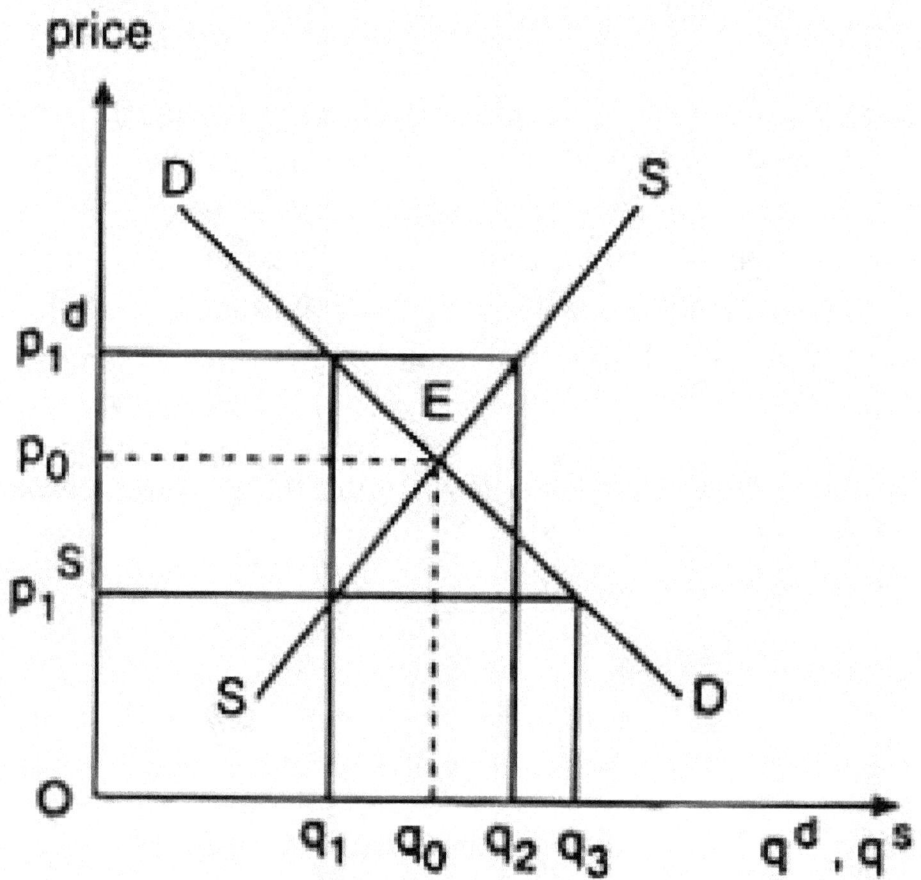

Fig. 1.17 Market equilibrium interms of demand price and supply price

Our economy is one of the most complex entities in the world. The world's monetary policy, currency exchange rates, and many other factors all come to play in determining global affairs and individual economies. This book is an examination of the role that supply and demand play across our entire society. Through this analysis, we hope to shed light on economic relationships and how they can be manipulated for profit or for political gain.

In order to understand economics, it's best to start by understanding what capitalism is. By understanding what capitalism is, we'll then be able to analyze its role within economics as well as how it has worked in recent years (or not). While there are multiple types of capitalism, such as Soviet-style communism or US-style capitalism, we will focus primarily on the latter and how it has played out across the globe.

The general consensus among economists is that supply and demand should be viewed as factors behind any economic activities. The world's financial balance, currency exchange rates, and the like all come into play to determine what products or services are available in our economy or not. Some view it as a factor, some view it as a game, and some focus more on the aspect of religion. When viewed in this way, supply and demand provide an explanation of how our economy operates.

Though supply and demand have always had an impact on economic decisions, the term "demand" defines how consumers decide which products or services they purchase. Demand is often thought of as something abstract, but at its core, it's simply the result of consumer choices. If consumers decide to purchase more beef than pork, or if they decide to consume less chicken than beef, then there will be less production for beef (or vice versa) and vice versa. Suppliers respond by adjusting their production accordingly to meet these varying demands.

Alternatively, "supply" speaks to how businesses decide which products or services they're going to offer. In the United States, this is referred to as the "demand-side." On this side of things, businesses have an idea of what products or services they'll need in order to meet consumer demand. If consumers want more iPads, then the business will have a strong incentive to produce more iPads. But if, in turn, these iPads are being produced at a higher price than what consumers are willing to pay for them, then consumers will have a strong incentive not to purchase these devices. This is the result of supply and demand playing out across our economy.

Throughout all of this, there's one thing that our economy lacks: control. While it's true that supply and demand do influence our economy, there is no way that our economy can dictate what goods or services are produced or consumed. That's where the government comes into play with its rules, laws, and regulations with regard to production and consumption. If businesses are not willing to abide by these rules, then the market will act on it with consequences.

A perfect example of this is how agriculture has acted in recent years. With the United States being one of the most agricultural-centric societies in all of history, there has been a strong focus on farming in recent years. This is completely understandable as a result of the need for food and resources. On the other hand, Americans have become more and more dependent on agriculture as a result of government requirements for it. If you take a look at the Supplemental Nutrition Assistance Program (SNAP) or food stamps, you can see proof of this.

SNAP has grown rapidly in recent years to the point where more than 47 million people are today (2014). There's also evidence that this number is growing, with some estimates suggesting that more than 75 million Americans will be receiving SNAP benefits by 2017 (Center on Budget and Policy Priorities). While there is no doubt that food stamps (and before that, food banks) do their part to help eliminate poverty and hunger, it has come at a cost.

With more people receiving SNAP benefits, there is more pressure on the agricultural industry to produce more foods. This puts additional strain on the US agricultural economy as a whole as farmers (and those who work in farming) struggle to meet this growing demand for food and resources. It's estimated that by 2050 we'll need 50% more food than we currently consume today just to keep our people fed. Whether we're able to keep up with this tremendous demand or not will speak volumes about our ability as a society and nation-state moving forward.

Food stamps and SNAP play an important role in addressing poverty and hunger, but when viewed from an economic standpoint, these programs give our government the ability to dictate what is produced and consumed within our economy. While it could be argued that this isn't a good thing (or a bad thing), it ultimately becomes a matter of perspective on how this should be viewed. With each passing year, you can see how market forces are driven by program requirements, quotas, and similar factors.

This is where demand comes into play with regard to supply-side economics. Genetically modified foods are yet another example of how government regulation has altered the food chain. While there is no question that GMOs should be regulated, the problem lies in the governments' lack of understanding of how to regulate them. While we can't say for sure what kind of impact GMOs have had on our agriculture economy, it's safe to say that they've played a role. It's also possible that they could play an even greater role in the years ahead.

It's safe to say that supply-side economics has its benefits as well as its drawbacks. Whether or not these drawbacks are important enough to warrant any changes remains to be seen, but something has got to give at some point. For example, economists have commented on how monetary policy has played a significant role in fluctuating commodity prices over the years. This alone suggests that monetary policy could have a negative impact on the production of goods and services.

On the other hand, supply-side economics has played a significant role in how our economy has changed in recent decades. In fact, supply-side economics is responsible for how many businesses operate today. While the consumer, or demand side, is always going to play a role in how our economy performs from one year to the next, there's no denying that supply-side economics plays a significant role. What will be interesting in the coming years is what happens when these two sides come into direct conflict with one another with regard to their respective roles within our society.

Chapter 10: Comparative Strength Analysis

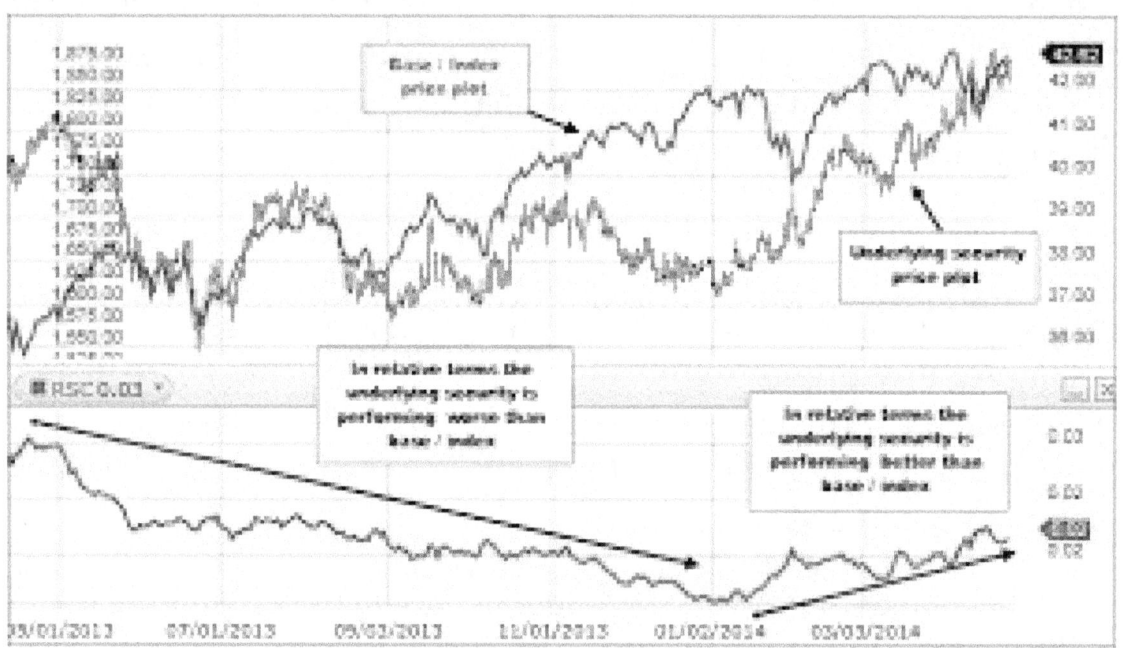

If you want to make the most of your workouts, it's important to understand how much weight you should be lifting, and how much weight you could lift. The latter will help establish a better baseline and determine the right time when returning from an injury. Understanding your personal strength levels can also improve the quality of your workouts and prevent reaching a level that is too heavy for training-based goals (e.g., muscle building or endurance). Answering this question does not require special equipment, and it can be completed within a day.

Below is a 3-step process to assess your relative strength levels. All you need is a set of weights that includes: 2.5 pounds (for women), 5 pounds (for women and men), and 10 pounds (for women and men) weights. This will enable you to calculate your personal peak weight percentage range for each exercise—a self-assessment benchmark that takes less than 1 minute per exercise.

Step 1: Perform the desired number of repetitions to Burnout (or failure)—

that is, the point at which additional repetitions would cause you to lose form or control over the weight being lifted.

Step 2: Calculate the percentage of your maximum weight that you were able to lift.

Ex. If you did 8 repetitions on the Lat Pulldown, you should still be able to do at least one more repetition with the 5-pound weight (your maximum weight). Therefore, your percentage of maximum weight = 8 × 5 / 8 = 60%.

The same process applies to the other exercises. The goal is not to calculate your maximum weight for each exercise but rather to identify, which weights fall into your range of strength (70–120% of your maximum). Once you have completed this self-assessment, keep track of your results in order to gauge progress over time.

Step 3: Determine multiples of your personal peak weight percentage by multiplying each of the percentages in Step 2 together. The combination will be the amount you would have been able to lift if you had a specific strength level. For example, a woman with a maximum-percentile 50% for chest press would take her 50% breakdown from Step 2, add the 5 lbs. she was tested with in Step 1, and multiply it by her personal peak weight percentage from Step 1 to get a combined 20 lbs. (5 lbs. × 0.50 + 5lbs × 0.60 = 20 lbs.). This would mean that she could have lifted 30 lbs. in one repetition if she had a 70% strength level instead.

Based on the example, a woman would have been able to lift 40 lbs. for 8 repetitions if she had a 70% strength level instead of a 50% strength level. So, her test results show her that she needs to increase her weight by 5 pounds in order to lift more weight for chest presses with a maximum-percentile of 50%. If she is able to increase this weight by 10 pounds per month (30 lbs. × 12 = 360 lbs.), then she will reach her next training goal within 12 months (360 / 0.5 = 720).

Chapter 11: Wyckoff Graphs Explained

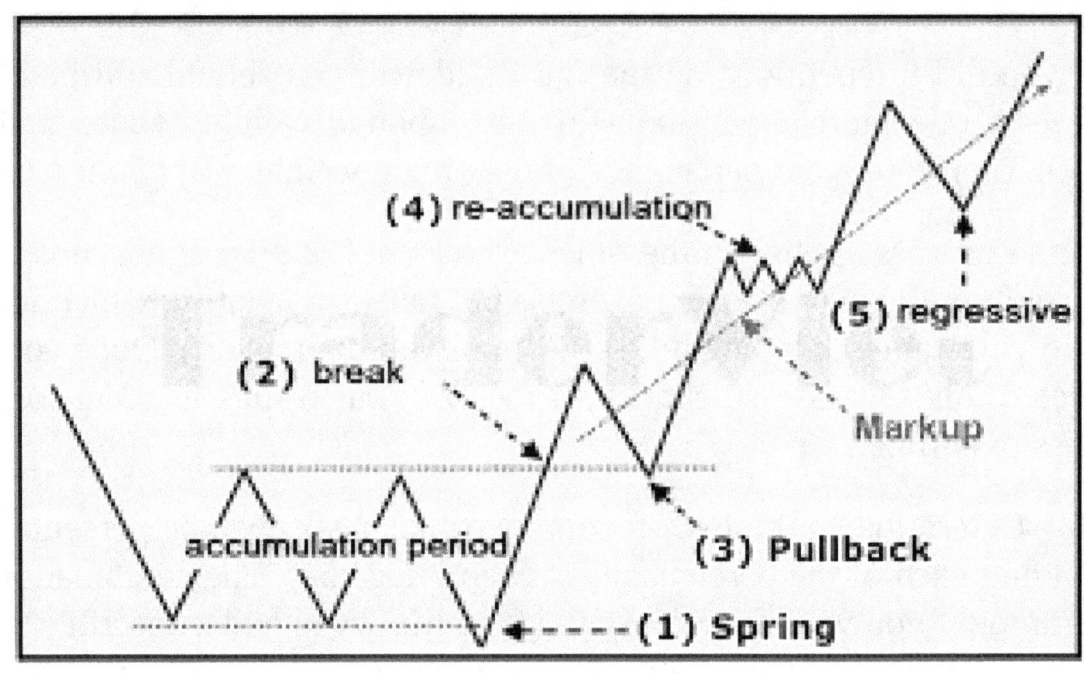

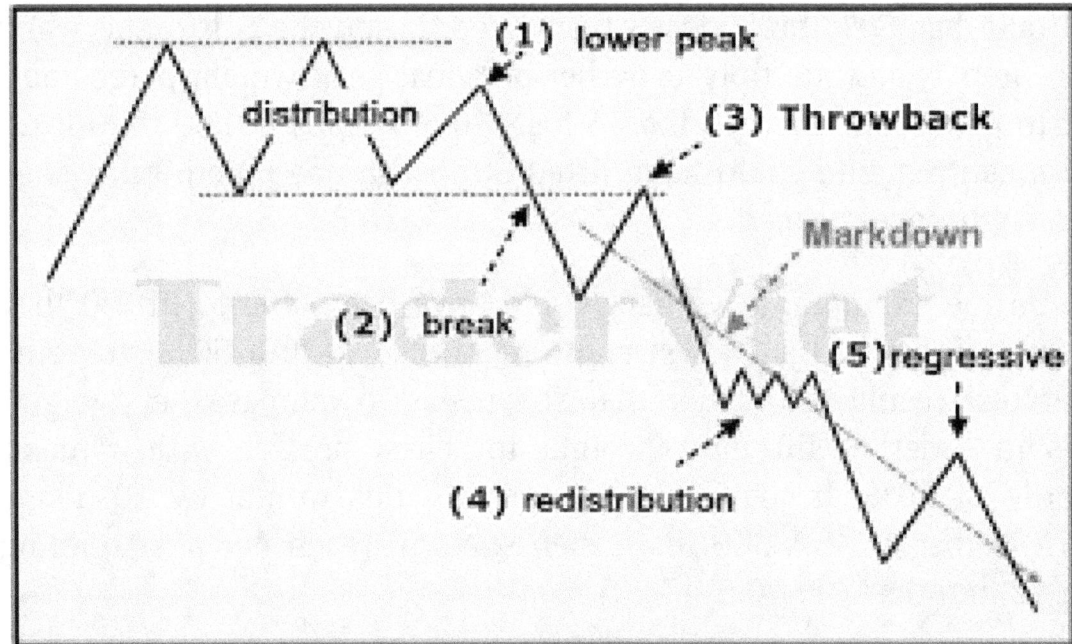

A Wyckoff is a type of technical analysis used to analyze stocks based on historical price performance. They are also known as "Wyckoff Vertical

Lines" or "Wyckoffs."

This book will teach you what a Wyckoff is, how it can be used, and, more importantly, why they're so popular among investors. Armed with this knowledge, you will be able to see the longer-term effects of trading Wyckoffs as well as anticipate their movements in real time.

On the surface, Wyckoffs appear very straightforward. They're based on a trend line that consists of three upward and downward price movement points. As Wyckoffs establish themselves as the dominant trend in a particular security's price, they can be used to identify primary directional moves as well as significant turning points. However, what makes these graphs so popular with investors is the reason why they were created in the first place; Wyckoff Graphs were designed to illustrate profit-taking and profit identification.

The idea is that investing is essentially a series of short-term trades that are gradually accumulated into long-term positions. In order to take the best advantage of a stock's potential, Wyckoff followers tend to buy at a low price and sell at a high price. They do this over and over again until they finally have enough to make a substantial investment.

Tracking trends may not be the flashiest way to invest. However, this approach puts less emphasis on trying to read stock charts or search for hidden patterns in customer sentiment. Instead, Wyckoff followers use historical information about how stocks have behaved in their infancy and then apply those precedents as they move into their adult life cycle. This is not a strategy for those who have a great deal of experience with the market. The Wyckoff followers' average trading experience is somewhere around just a few years.

One of the most important benefits that comes from the use of Wyckoff Indicators involves protection from market volatility. As Wyckoffs move, they can indicate significant changes in stock prices as well as identify those who buy low and sell high at the right times. In this sense, they can be said to protect investors from common mistakes or issues that may arise as markets fluctuate over time. This is the reason why so many traders have used them over time to gain a greater understanding of share market movements.

A common complaint about Wyckoff graphs is that they are somewhat subjective. It's essential to note that this isn't to say that these are useless, just that they're not 100% objective. The Wyckoff followers are simply basing their apparent success on history, not science or mathematics. They begin with an idea of how a particular stock has performed prior to the current trend, then implement this information into their trading strategies. More often than not, the result will later show itself as an improvement in profit over time by following the same basic formula established early on by stock market expert Charles Wyckoff himself.

This doesn't mean that a Wyckoff Graph is easily faked. There's a certain amount of logic and rationale behind the strategy, which is why it's possible to teach a new trader how to spot a fake. Though, there can be some confusion over which specific line should be used as the Wyckoff indicator if your own trading history differs from the history recorded by others.

In addition to being able to use Wyckoff Indicators as an investment tool, they also have practical uses as well as advantages within one's everyday life. They're commonly used as a way to assess risk based on past events or expectations about future outcomes. So, suppose you're wondering whether or not you should take that vacation, invest in that new business idea, or even buy a new car. In that case, Wyckoffs can help you gauge the potential risk associated with each investment opportunity.

One of the biggest criticisms about Wyckoff's approach to trading is that it takes several years to build any form of significant profit. This is non-negotiable. It's not like when trading stocks online where one minute you're in the red then in the black simply by clicking on an option to trade. It takes time for Wyckoffs to become profitable; sometimes only months, but for others, it may take years. Therefore, this strategy isn't ideal for people who are looking for quick returns right away.

The good news, however, is that Wyckoff Indicators are far more important to follow rather than simply focus on long-term profits. While it may take several years to build up a significant amount of money, these graphs can aid you in making the right decisions about what to do with them once they're gained. If you recognize that buying at a low price and then selling at a high price is the way to go, then you'll end up with your money in better shape than if you'd invested in an index fund or traded stocks trading at overpaid prices.

As long as you understand the importance of this, you can begin to appreciate the value of these graphs as an investment tool for your everyday life. They are especially important if you are considering getting involved in a business venture or making major purchases. Wyckoff followers will also counsel their clients to stick to their course of action rather than missing out on what could be a profitable endeavor.

Wyckoff followers will tell their clients that they're not out to make money on one day's trading decisions. They simply want to use past trends and experience as a base for what will eventually be profitable trades. This is especially important when it comes to longer-term investments, such as buying a home, purchasing a new car, or even starting a business. As with day-trading, their goal is to buy low and sell high at the right time rather than get caught up in the hype of the moment.

When you're thinking about starting a business venture for yourself, you want to make sure that it will be profitable enough that it's worth your time and effort when you're ready to sell. That's why using Wyckoff indicators is so important in the long run. While they may seem boring or lead to disappointing results over time, they truly are the key to making the right decisions with your money.

You've probably heard the phrase "buy low, sell high" at one time or another in your life. But how difficult is that to actually do? The truth is that you can buy low and sell high, but if you're not paying attention, you just might end up losing money in the process. Fortunately, there are people who've devised systems to help us navigate the stock market in order to profit no matter what happens. And one of those systems is called Wyckoff Analysis. This can be used when trading stocks online or even when making decisions about your personal finances.

There's a reason why Wyckoff Indicators were popular and recognized for many years in the stock market. It's because they work. Just like when you've been losing in the stock market or in your business venture, you don't want to give up and sit around and complain about it. You need to buy back into the market and try again. But this time, you'll be armed with the knowledge that can help you profit no matter what happens.

The people who started the Wyckoff Method of investing were looking at how people invested in property before there were property loans or mortgages available to buy. They noticed that people were buying a house and then selling it for a profit before the house was even completed. This also meant they could get money from their homes while they lived in them, but when they sold them to move to another property, they'd profit from it. They tried to take this concept and apply it to stocks, and it worked like a charm.

The Wyckoff Method of investing analyzes how stocks will move by forecasting the movement of stocks based on past data. The method doesn't predict the future movements of any particular stock; instead, it looks at the movement of the overall market and makes predictions about what will happen next. The Wyckoff Method is effective because of the way it uses history to predict future stock movements.

What Does It Take to Study Wyckoff Indicators?

The truth of the matter is that you don't need an expensive degree or formal training to use Wyckoff Indicators and make money. The benefit of this is that if you fail, it doesn't cost much money. If you succeed, you'll make enough profit from stocks to cover your initial investment and then some. This means it's easy for anyone to do - regardless of the amount of money they have in their accounts or whether or not they're an expert trader.

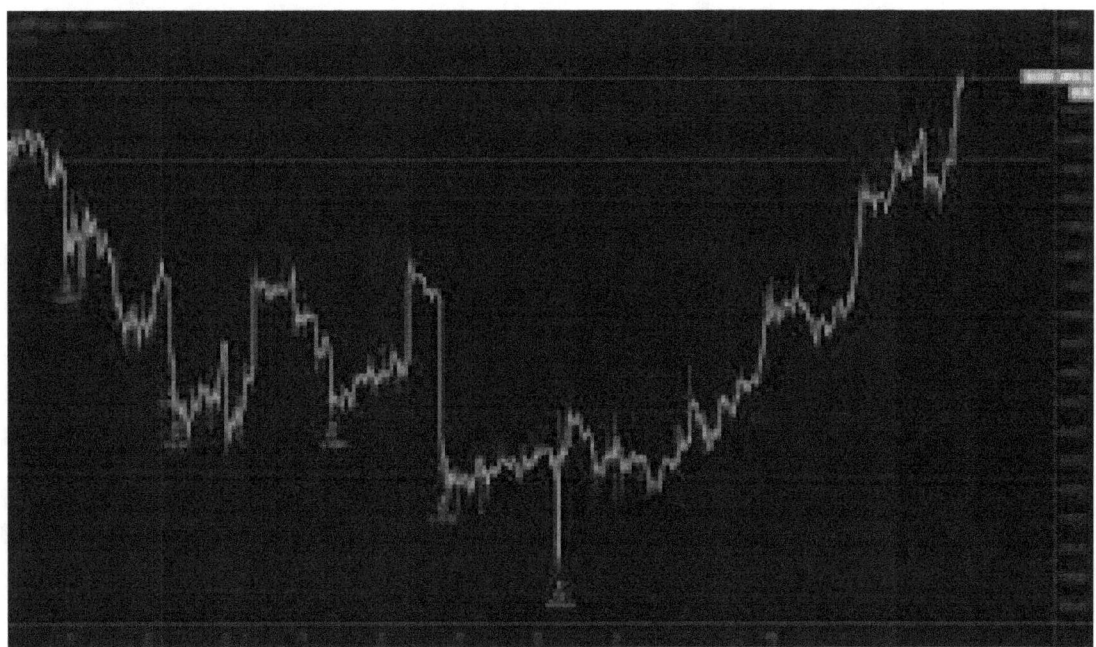

What You Can Do with the Wyckoff Method of Investing

The Wyckoff Method doesn't just apply to stock market investing. It can be used for other types of investments as well. One of the most common ways this is used is when buying a car, real estate, or even investing in cars on lease-to-own. With any of these types of investments, investors need to know how to make sure they are buying low and selling high in order to make the most money possible.

Wyckoff Indicators are one of the best ways for people to make sure they are making the right moves when investing their money. It's not difficult to understand and use and can help you make profits in any one of the above-mentioned forms of investment. If you want to make sure you're making the most out of your investments, Wyckoff Indicators are a must for your investment toolbox.

Chapter 12: 3 Fundamental Laws

> **The Three Laws**
>
> - 1) Supply and Demand - Why Prices Rise and Fall
>
>   When demand is greater than supply, prices will rise, and when supply is greater than demand, prices will fall. Here the analyst studies the relationship between supply and demand using price and volume over time as found on a bar chart.
>
> - 2) Effort vs. Results - Strength of a Move, by Bar and by Swing
>
>   Divergences and disharmonies between volume and price often presage a change in the direction of the price trend. Volume Spread analysis & Comparative Relative Strength.
>
> - 3) Cause & Effect - Market Structure & Phases
>
>   In order to have an effect you must first have a cause, and that effect will be in proportion to the cause. This law's operation can be seen working in the force of accumulation or distribution within a trading range, working itself out in the subsequent move out of that trading range. Price and figure chart counts can be used to measure the cause and project the extent of its effect.

The price of an asset can never just go up in a straight line. Rather, it goes through different cycles that repeat themselves over and over again. These cycles come from the 3 laws that Dr. W.D. Gann and Dr. R.N.E Wyckoff first stated: The Law of Cause and Effect, The Law of Effort versus Result, and The Law of Cause and Effect in Reverse.

The Law of Cause and Effect is the most basic law of cause and effect. It states that "every action has an equal and opposite reaction," which is also known as Newton's Third Law. While this specific law deals with physics, it applies to economics because everything in life is connected, such that what you do affects other people's (or person's) lives.

The second law dictates that there must be an effort put for every reaction before any result can be seen. This applies to everything, not just economics. When you want to succeed at something, you need to put in an effort (some kind of work) before you can see any result (the end goal, for instance). If one were to put in no effort, they would not be able to achieve their goals.

The third law is the opposite of the second law. It states that for every effort, there is a cause (which causes the action), but for every "because" there must be an effect (which causes the reaction). This is also good news because it means that results do not necessarily appear instantly; behind every action, there will always be an effect somewhere. In other words, if you put an effort in order, there will be a reaction where the effort was placed.

The above three laws of economics can be applied to practically anything. The 3 laws of economics can be applied to a person's life as a whole or a business as a whole. Just as with investing, understanding these laws would give one an advantage in the market because one can move other people and get results from them. Getting up in the morning and thinking about how to move others so they will get the same result would help get what you want from them. To get school better grades, one should study hard so that they get higher test scores.

The 3 laws of economics are the foundation on which W.D. Gann built his theories of stock market forecasting, which can be found in "The Tower of Basel." A short summary of the principles can be found below:

- Prices move in cycles. This cycle is the Ideal Bar Cycle (IBC) and is described here (starting January 2006). The price moves upward; then it moves through a period of decline; then it again moves upward; then it again moves through a period of decline; and so on… this pattern repeats indefinitely. This is the law of effort versus result… you'll need to put in more effort during times where prices are moving downward than you will during an upward movement.
- The major advances in price occur at times of accumulation (i.e., the stock market is growing) or times of exhaustion (i.e., stocks are declining).
- There are cycles in the price of individual stocks; prices move up, then down; then up, then down.

The IBC is a hypothetical process that describes what the real-world experience would look like if stock market prices did follow an ideal cycle, complete with price advances and declines (filled in with gaps when no price movement can be found in shares trading at any given time). The IBC consists of 3 steps: accumulation, adjustment to new supply/demand factors, and exhaustion… which cycle over and over again. The IBC is not to be confused with the price movement of an individual stock, even though parts of the IBC may coincide with parts of an individual stock's price cycle.

Gann believed that there was a certain point where one could find a "climax" or "turning point" in the IBC, particularly when prices moved downward. Often, during a downward move in prices, this turning point can be found by looking at 2 consecutive peaks/troughs and finding the highest peak/lowest trough between those 2 points. This is when the IBC hits its climax. The climax marks the moment in time that prices are at their lowest. The IBC then begins to rise again… in a process known as "adjustment." This process of adjustment will continue until accumulation begins again… in a process known as "accumulation."

Gann's theories on the IBC were based upon the idea that prices moved in cycles or sine waves, much like a wave on a seashell representing ocean waves. Gann compared these waves to ocean waves, saying that there are high points, low points, and turns in the stock market sine wave. Gann also stated that it took a period of two to three years for the stock market to reach a peak and another period of two to three years for the stock market to reach a trough. For example, when the NASDAQ reached its peak in 2000, it took 2–3 years for prices to return to their preceding peak (which occurred in early 2000). Gann also stated that when the NASDAQ hit its lowest point during 2008, prices would not return to that low point (and probably wouldn't even come close) until sometime after 2016.

Although much of his work was based on cycles, Gann did hold some important concepts of his own. Regarding this part of his work, John Embry writes: "W.D. Gann was a very intelligent man, but some of his theories were a little far-fetched. He thought that the bull market in 1929 was going to last forever, and there were some other things he said that didn't make a lot of sense… But whether you believe in cycles or not, it doesn't matter. The important thing is to find your own price cycle."

Chapter 13: How to Trade Applying the Wyckoff Methodology—Made Easy

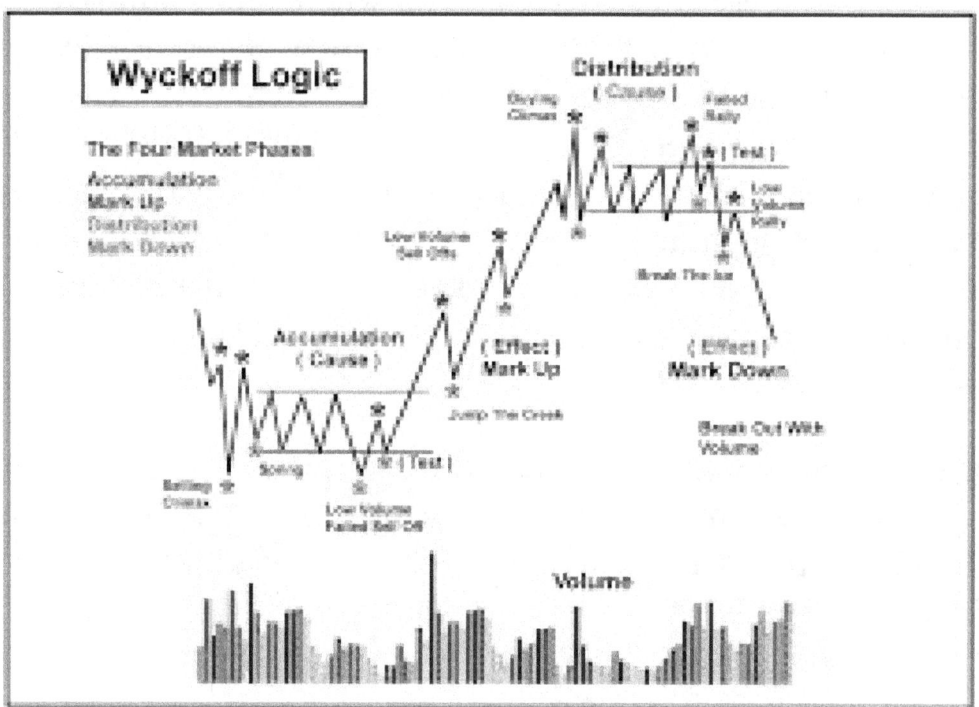

The Wyckoff Methodology is a trading methodology for investing. It's been around since 1940 and has been used by all types of traders, from long-term to day traders. In this book, we'll take you through the process step by step so that you can apply the Wyckoff Methodology to any market just as easily as an expert would!

In order to trade successfully with this method, you have to have a good understanding of your investment environment and be able to execute trades yourself or via a broker or bank.

For Trend Trading

Be able to trend trade in either direction, i.e., buy and sell the majors and minor averages and the Dow stocks. Be able to trend trade in an intermediate-term time frame, i.e., 4–10 days, depending on the design of the Wyckoff Methodology that you're using for your specific style of investing. Understand how to identify a reversal in the market. Be able to trade reversals either at support or resistance. Understand how to identify support and resistance using trend lines, retracements, channels, and/or pullbacks. Be able to identify the different Wyckoff price patterns that are available for trading trends, i.e., trending markets or reversals in the market. Be able to use the Order Book feature on your charting software when entering and exiting trades or when placing stop-loss orders in order to exit before a possible threshold level is hit.

For Counter-Trend Trading

Be able to counter-trend trade in either direction in an intermediate-term time frame, i.e., 4–10 days, depending on the design of the Wyckoff Methodology that you're using for your specific style of investing. Understand how to identify a reversal in the market. Be able to counter-trend trade either at support or resistance. Understand how to find buying opportunities when prices are below support or selling opportunities when prices are above resistance. Be able to identify the different Wyckoff price patterns that are available for trading counter-trends, i.e., ranging markets or reversals in the market. Be able to use the Order Book feature on your charting software when entering and exiting trades or when placing stop-loss orders in order to exit before a possible threshold level is hit.

For Trend Trading Using the Wyckoff Method

Here are the main rules to follow:

- Always buy strength and sell weakness. That's right; there's only one way to trade trend reversal patterns, which are counter-trends in your favor that turn into a newly established trend in the same direction, then sell at support or sell at resistance. When you do this, you're driving weak longs out by selling at resistance and driving strong shorts out by selling at support.
- Always trade the trend. If you're in a trending market, you should be in a long position if it's going up or in a short position if it's going down. If it's not in an established trend, then you should wait for it to become one before entering a trade.
- Don't try to pick tops or bottoms. I'm sure most of you have tried to pick tops or bottoms, which is impossible anyway. Just try to get into positions after your trading conditions are met so that you will have the best probability of success with your trades.
- Always have risk management controls set up correctly for optimal trading results. To have these controls in place, you have to have the proper rules in place. If you don't, then your risk is too high with potential blow-ups that can occur when your rules are broken.
- Always cut your losses short and let your winners run. This is one of the best rules in trading; however, you must make sure that you use a protective stop-loss order when you enter a trade in order to get out safely before any possible reversal in the market takes place.

For Counter-Trend Trading Using the Wyckoff Method

When trading counter-trends using the Wyckoff method, here are some of the Rules of Trading:

- Always buy weakness and sell strength when counter-trend trading. That's right; you're going with the trend as it is now as opposed to looking to try and pick tops or bottoms. The less time you spend trying to pick tops or bottoms, the more time you have to spend focusing on how to execute trades properly.
- Always trade counter-trends in an intermediate-term time frame, i.e., 4–10 days, depending on the design of the Wyckoff Methodology that you're using for your specific style of investing.
- Always use a protective stop-loss order when entering a trade in order to get out safely before any possible reversal in the market takes place.

When trading in a ranging market using the Wyckoff method, here are some of the Rules of Trading:

- Don't try to pick tops or bottoms. This is difficult for any trader when they're in a ranging market. When you try to pick tops or bottoms, you'll lose more than win, and the odds are against you when trying to make this work.
- Be prepared for counter-trends either up or down, which could be larger in degree than that of the current trend. You can expect ranging markets to be volatile, and that's why we trade them only when we have a high probability of success with our trades. This is another reason why you should always use protective stop-loss orders when trading in a ranging market.
- Always have your risk management controls in place for optimal trading results. You will need to have your rules in place for you to be able to have the proper risk management controls. If you don't, then your risk is too high with potential blow-ups that can occur

- when your rules are broken.
- Always cut your losses short and let your winners run.

They say if it isn't broke, don't fix it, and I think this holds true for most traders as they work with one or more price action patterns from the master trader Richard Wyckoff. I've been trading and educating traders for nearly 10 years, and it's always surprised me how many traders and investors want to reinvent the wheel and learn how to trade using "their own method" or "their own pattern set." Well, suppose you're able to go back in time and meet Richard Wyckoff himself. In that case, I'm sure you would hear him tell you that his methods were based on money management, time frames, proper risk management controls (rules), statistical probabilities (do the math), and market-based order flow. If one of these elements is missing from your trading or investing approach, then you're taking unnecessary risks that could lead to a loss of capital.

Chapter 14: How to Trade and Invest in Stocks and Bonds

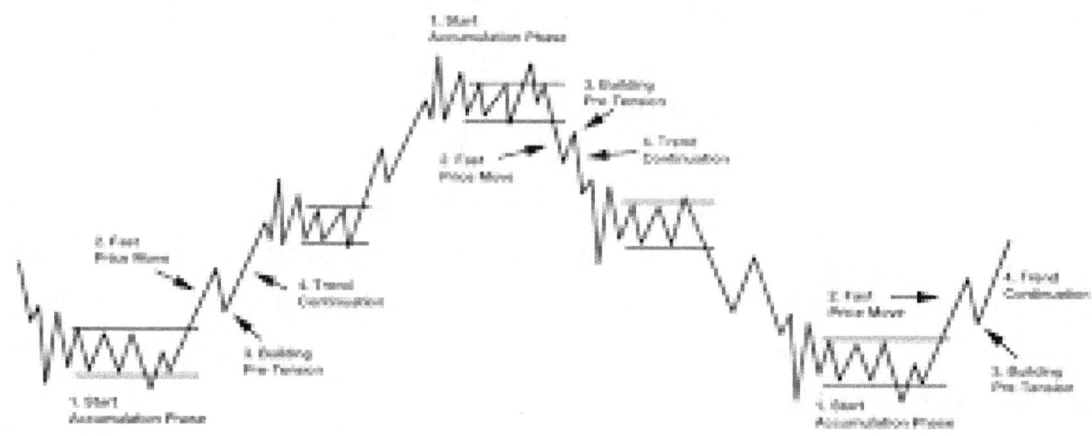

Investing or trading in stocks and bonds is a core part of the financial market. With this book, we will give you a little background on how these marketplaces work. Learn about stock exchanges and how they distribute broker's fees, as well as the fundamentals of stocks, bonds, and ETFs. This can help you maximize your profit margins or hedge against unforeseen risks in the future. Let us show you what investing in these markets means for your financial security! We're here to answer all those pesky questions about stocks and bonds that may have been keeping you up at night.

The stock market is a marketplace where investors can trade financial products such as stocks, bonds, options, and futures. It is a big system that moves billions of dollars every year. This guide will provide a broad overview of the markets and how companies use these markets to tap into billions of dollars.

Our goal is to give you a basic understanding of how the stock (and bond) market works and what you need to know about trading in these different instruments.

We will also touch on investing in ETFs (Exchange-Traded Funds) similar to stocks but trade like an index fund or mutual fund. You don't have to worry about commissions or commission rollover fees with ETFs since they are traded like an index fund.

The stock market is the basis of our economy. It is where businesses endeavor to grow bigger by expanding into new markets and developing new products or services that will increase their profits.

This allows companies to grow bigger and expand to other cities, states, and countries. This gives them the opportunity to appeal to more people who can contribute to their value, thereby increasing it.

The stock market also serves as a source of funding for these companies. Money to start a business comes from investors who trust that the risk of investment is worth the reward. If they see promise in its products and services, they will want to get in on it.

The stock market helps you navigate the risks of investing. This is because if you let your investments grow too large before selling, then you may end up with a lot less money in your account when the time comes to sell or an even bigger loss. To prevent that from happening, the brokerage firm will give you an estimate when there are large movements in stock prices. These estimates are called stops. They will tell you when to sell in case the price drops, and you don't want to take a loss.

With this in mind, we believe that in order to minimize losses and maximize gains; it is important for investors to practice cutting their losses and letting their profits ride.

Shares of stock represent part ownership of a company. The value of these shares depends on how much people are willing to pay for the company's future earnings potential.

Investors buy shares with the hope that they will earn a profit when they sell them. If the price goes up, then so does the return on investment. If the price goes down, it can cost an investor money if they are unable to sell shares at a reasonable price.

This uncertainty is one of the greatest risks for investors. However, there are ways to mitigate risk by following fundamental analysis and technical analysis.

The stock market is broken up into several different sectors, including energy, industry, financials, technology, healthcare, consumer discretionary, and consumer staples. These sectors are like an iceberg as they represent only a small portion of the market, but what they lack in size makes up for diversity.

With this diversity comes the chance to earn greater profits. Because of how many different types of companies there are, there's always the potential to find one that will work out for you. It all depends on your analysis of certain trends and factors that go into value price prediction.

Bonds are debt securities issued by governments or companies. Investors purchase bonds to raise money for their current or future projects or needs. Investors can also buy bonds even if they don't plan to use them for raising money.

Bonds take on different forms. Some bond types include:

Bonds Issued by Companies

What is a bond? A bond is a security issued by a company to raise money for its projects. When the company repays the loan, it will redeem (i.e., return) the original face value of the bond to the investor at maturity. Note that this doesn't mean that the investor will get back all his or her money at that time, but only that he or she will get his or her principal back.

The investor must be aware of how much bonds pay and what they pay when it comes time to redeem them accordingly.

The value of the bond will vary with interest rates. If interest rates go up, then bond prices (and yields) will fall. If interest rates go down, then bond prices will rise.

Corporate bonds are generally considered to be lower risk than government bonds because they are backed by the creditworthiness of the corporation issuing them. The greater the financial strength of the issuing company, generally speaking, the lower the risk is to an investor in terms of getting his or her money back.

However, corporate bonds may also be riskier than government bonds because they can default if their projects fail or profit margins decline.

Companies get paid for the products and services they sell. This money is used to pay for fixed assets such as plant and equipment, but it is also used to pay the debt. Companies usually borrow money from banks or sell bonds to raise this capital.

When a company sells bonds, it agrees to pay back the bondholder at a later time, usually after five years. The investor gains interest on the loan, so if the company is successful in its business, then its success will benefit the bondholder in terms of both interest payments and when he or she cashes out at maturity.

The borrower pays interest on top of the principal with every payment. This payment is called coupon interest or simply coupon payments. This is usually a fixed rate, which means the bondholder knows exactly how much he or she will receive each quarter until maturity.

Some bonds pay a floating rate of interest, which means the rate can change depending on the performance of another source.

Inflation is also considered a risk in relation to bonds because, when inflation increases, bondholders can expect their principal balance to decrease when they cash out. This is because the interest rates paid on the bond are based on a certain inflation rate, which is often expressed as an index.

Therefore, the interest payments are made at discounted values that are lower than the actual rate of inflation. This means that when it comes time to redeem or cash out, the investor will only receive back their principal.

You do not own a piece of a corporation when you invest in stocks. Instead, you're an owner of a company's stock (which gives its owners voting rights). The value of these shares depends on how much people are willing to pay for their future earnings potential.

The stock market is broken up into several different sectors, including energy, industry, financials, technology, healthcare, consumer discretionary, and consumer staples. These sectors are like an iceberg as they represent only a small portion of the market.

Some of the most common markets include:

Stocks are also divided into different industry groups, including Consumer Discretionary, Consumer Staples, Health Care, Energy, Transportation/Utilities, and Industrials.

These industries contain thousands of companies that serve millions of investors worldwide. The growth (or lack thereof) in any one industry can affect pricing as well as pricing movements across different industries as a whole.

Price movements on stocks depend on supply-demand, news, and, more importantly, the overall state of the economy. This is because stocks are investments people make in corporations to produce profits. Therefore, if the economy is doing better (or worse), then stock prices will react according to investor sentiment. If people are optimistic, then they will buy stocks and drive-up prices. If they're pessimistic about the future prospects of a company, then they'll sell their shares and drive down prices.

Companies can also offer dividends (a portion of the profit that has been reinvested into the company). This depends on how well a company is doing and what its management decides. Investors can also cash out with options trading as well as selling their shares on secondary markets such as stock exchanges, exchanges, and alternative trading markets.

There are many different types of investment instruments investors can choose from. They include stocks, bonds, foreign exchange, commodities, currencies, precious metals, derivative contracts, and options.

Stocks are the most common investment instrument available because they're easy to trade and the most liquid. Stocks are also easily traded at brokerage houses online or across many different venues. However, bonds are traditionally considered to be a very safe investment because they typically yield higher rates than stocks.

Bonds must be held until their maturity date. For instance, you cannot sell an American debt security (bond) before its maturity date if you want your principal returned to you. Banks offer many different bond products for investors to choose from. The most common include US Treasuries, corporate bonds, and municipal bonds.

Some bonds are considered to be riskier because their interest rates are lower than other bonds. These include high-yield or "junk" bonds. They have a higher chance of default because they have a lower credit rating from a major credit agency such as Standard & Poor's, Moody's, and Fitch. Therefore, the chance of repayment is not as guaranteed.

There are many different investment strategies available to investors who want to hedge their investments against risk. The most common include investing in funds, investing in stocks or mutual funds, investing in ETFs or exchange-traded funds, and using derivatives.

Funds are commonly used as a way to diversify your investment portfolio. Funds usually include many different securities, such as bonds, mutual funds, exchange-traded funds, and debt instruments.

Investing in mutual funds is a great way to manage risk because the fund manager will buy and sell the securities for you. He or she will also make adjustments throughout the year depending on market conditions. However, this does not mean that investing in mutual funds is risk-free. It is very common for bonds to default, so you can lose money over time.

ETFs are very similar to mutual funds, but are traded on stock exchanges instead of brokerage accounts. They are also considered to be another form of diversifying your portfolio by keeping it liquid. Investors can also use derivatives to hedge against risk. These include swap agreements, options, futures, and forward contracts.

Derivatives allow you to make a contract without knowing the exact price. In this case, you are essentially making a bet on the price of something. Just like other securities, derivatives can be bought and sold. The two main types of derivative contracts include futures and options.

Futures contracts allow investors to lock in a certain price at a set point in time. For example, if you're an investor who believes that oil prices will go up, then you may purchase futures contracts for $50 per barrel at $60 per barrel right now. If oil prices go up to $70 per barrel, then the contract will automatically payout one hundred dollars at the end of the contract term. Futures are also commonly used by commodity traders to hedge against risk.

Options are another form of derivatives that allow you to bet on an asset without assuming any risk. If you believe that a stock will fall, you can use options to predict how long it will be until it goes up or down. At the end of your contract, there will be a payout depending on what that stock does. Using options is best suited for investors who have more experience because options are very complicated.

You can also use your credit card to invest in these securities if you're a big spender. It is a good idea to research which online brokers have the best track record of turning a profit from their customers' trades.

You can also use options trading to hedge your investments against risk. Options offer you leverage, which means that you can get more out of a trade than you put in. If this happens, then great! But if it doesn't, then this will come back to haunt you later. For traders who don't have enough time to research everything, options trading is a good way to make short-term trades.

A common rule of thumb for how much you should save in your emergency fund is around six months' worth of expenses. However, this depends on what type of job you have.

If you cannot save at least three- or four-months' worth of expenses, then it would be best to get an interest-bearing savings account. This way, your money will start earning some cash for you while you're at work.

Be sure to find an FDIC-insured bank if you're going to keep your money in a savings account because this means that your cash is guaranteed up to $250,000 per bank. The current interest rate for savings accounts is around one percent, but it varies by bank, so be sure to check.

If you save enough, then at least you can get by if something happens. It is always a good idea to have several months' worth of expenses in your savings account because you never know when something will happen to disrupt your income.

An investment account is different from a savings account because the FDIC does not insure it. If something were to happen that could potentially harm your investments, then at least you can recover some of your losses. The best way for you to recover money, in this case, is by using stop-loss orders.

A stop-loss order allows you to sell any security at a pre-determined price. This means that if your investments take a massive hit, you can sell the securities at low prices and use the money to pay off other debts.

Stop-loss orders can be very helpful if you're not sure what to do. It is important to remember that this is not a guaranteed way of making money, so you should always think twice before using them.

If you have a larger debt to your name, your savings and investments will be split between debts and investments. You should use stop-loss orders because they will help you sell securities you no longer need and use the money to cover debts.

It is essential to keep track of your expenses because, over time, they can add up. The average American household spends about $11,000 per year on their miscellaneous expenses.

The problem with all of these expenses is that they can be very hard to predict or control. For example, how will you know if the price of milk is going to go up? If it does, then you should buy more since this will save you money in the long run.

A better solution is to take all of your miscellaneous expenses and put them into a single account. Whenever the account starts running low, you will have to plan ahead for extra spending.

The two best things that you can do for your investments are to get started early and make sure that you stay disciplined. When you start investing, the younger you are, the more experienced you will be when market conditions aren't perfect. And since nobody can predict what will happen in the future, it's important to stay disciplined no matter how much money is at stake. If everything else fails, then take this advice into consideration because it could save your life.

The most common blunder made by most investors is purchasing stocks without understanding why. And the most common reason is that the stock market seems out of trend or unpredictable. This can be dangerous because it can lead to panic selling, giving rise to extreme volatility.

The best way for you to avoid making these mistakes is to adhere to strict investing principles. Diversification is the most crucial guideline you should follow. This means that if one investment goes into a downturn, then you will still have other investments that are not affected.

When making your investments, make sure that you don't put all of your money in one place. If this happens, then one security could all-of-a-sudden become too much for your portfolio. You should use different types of funds for different purposes.

For example, you might have a riskier fund for your emergency fund, a more conservative one for your retirement, and a very safe one for your children.

It is also important to have a plan in place in order to avoid unnecessary risks. You should look over this strategy every so often in order to make sure that it still makes sense in terms of risk and reward.

If you build a strong safety net, then when the worst happens, you will be able to fall back on something that has been prepared just in case. When this is done right, then the anxiety of falling into debt will be avoided.

Investors who are dedicated enough can use options trading to manage their portfolio risk. This means that they can sell options to protect themselves against loss. But this should be done with caution because it could reduce the odds of success.

This is why it is important that you fully understand your investments because this will help you make better decisions. This way, you can feel more confident in your decisions and manage the risks to your portfolio. If you do not, then you are bound to make mistakes that could cost you dearly.

Another thing that investors need to understand is how to time the market. If the market makes a big move one way or another, then it's important for you to recognize what has changed. If there are new developments, then there may be an opportunity for you in this situation.

When you time the market, it is important to be patient and not overreact. If you see a price movement that could benefit your portfolio, then you need to take some time to consider how to take advantage of this situation.

Even if the market seems like it is going nowhere, you should still be able to find opportunities. There are always new businesses that are being formed, and there will always be new people entering the workforce. The stock market goes up and down all the time, so you should look for these dips in order to get in at low prices.

If you are new to investing, then stay away from penny stocks until you know what they are all about. If these stocks have a bad reputation, then you should stay away from them. If you do decide to take a chance on one of these penny stocks, then keep in mind that nobody can predict whether or not they will go up or down.

If it is your first time buying penny stocks, then you should minimize the amount of risk that you are taking by looking for companies that have been around for a long time. You can use a service like Y charts to help avoid a lot of the risks associated with investing in these companies.

When it comes to trading options, make sure that you never place too much at stake at any one time. If the market falls, then your options could be worth less than they were before.

Even worse, you could lose all of your money. So, it is always better to keep this in mind and always think about your situation before you decide to do anything drastic.

Investors who are looking for quick returns will oftentimes turn towards penny stocks. This is because they can earn large returns in a short amount of time. The flip side is that they may not understand the risks involved with these kinds of investments.

The reason why these kinds of stocks are appealing is that the companies don't make much money, and there is not much information about them. This way, you can sell your shares to somebody else for a lot more than you paid for them. But this could be risky if not analyzed correctly. If you are going to invest in penny stocks, then you should have the information necessary to make educated decisions.

There are some investors who use charts in order to time the market. These investors believe that they can predict how the market is going to move. They believe that most traders are following this trend, but most don't understand that the trading patterns are random. If you decide to use this strategy, then make sure that you do not fall into the trap of thinking that these patterns will always repeat themselves.

While it may be true that there is a trend with trading patterns, your family will suffer if you use this strategy because it could lead to overconfidence. Put too much faith into this strategy, and you will end up losing money that you don't have in the first place.

The most important thing to remember about investing in penny stocks is that it requires a high level of risk. You have to be really careful when investing in these kinds of companies. If you are going to invest, then it is important to do so with a full understanding of the risks that come with your investment.

If you want to save on fees, then look into consolidating your investments through a custodian service. This way, when you have a large portfolio, just call one institution and let them handle all of your investments for you.

The trick to picking a custodian service is to find one that has a low fee schedule. This way, you can build up your portfolio and still save as much money as possible.

There are many different factors that will help you determine if a custodian service is worth it. The first thing that you need to look at is the amount of fees involved. Also, do they charge commission for trades? Do they charge extra fees for their services? These are all things that should be considered before making a choice.

These factors will help you make an informed decision and be able to choose one of the best custodian services out there.

The best thing about these services is that they will help you understand how the market works and may even help you pick some good penny stocks. If you use a service like this, you will learn how to trade options with greater success.

You should always use a low-fee stockbroker if your goal is to limit your fees as much as possible.

As with the last point that we mentioned, keep in mind that there are many different factors that should be considered before investing in particular stocks. It is important for you to look into the company that the stockbroker works for because this could have an effect on your overall experience.

You should also look into the different types of products that are available for trade. Do they offer options? Do they offer penny stocks? When you are looking into picking a stockbroker, then you should consider their reputation as well.

Also, do they make trades based on technical analysis, or is it based on something else? All of these things should be considered to help give you an idea about the quality of work that they will provide.

You can save money by using a discount broker that charges lower fees to retail investors. This way, you will be able to avoid paying high commissions to realize your investment potential.

You may realize that some discount brokers charge more than others. That is why it is important to do your research before choosing one. You want to find one that offers low fees and convenient services.

The most important thing is to determine the reliability of the discount broker that you are looking at. First, you will want to look into their background. Are they regulated? Do they have a good reputation? These are all things that you will want to look into before making a final decision.

Chapter 15: Correlation between the Wyckoff Methodology and Real Estate Market Trends

The Wyckoff methodology is a stock market trading strategy that can be applied to almost any type of security. It's mostly used in the securities of commodity traders, but it can also be applied to real estate investments.

There are two basic rules that one should always keep in mind when applying the Wyckoff Methodology to real estate investments. The first rule is "buy low sell high"—in other words, buy stocks or properties when prices are low and sell them off when prices are high. The second rule that we will talk about is "buy and hold" —keep your investments in the same properties for a certain period of time.

The Wyckoff Methodology is very simple and can be understood easily by anyone with this great ability to recognize patterns. It has been used successfully by investors for many years now, and it is very effective in almost all scenarios. A trader using the Wyckoff Methodology would only need to use reliable information, and they will already know which stocks to buy and which ones to sell off.

The Wyckoff Methodology works well when applied correctly; however, it may not work well. For example, during the early 1990s, there were many investors who did not apply this methodology correctly, and they ended up losing a lot of money.

Real estate investing is mostly based on emotions, and it can be difficult for people to apply this method because they're not really sure when their investments should be bought and which ones should be sold, or at least this is what they think. The Wyckoff Methodology also does not work for all markets since it only works well in commodity trading such as stocks and oil, but it can still work in real estate because it's more of an actual asset rather than just an investment stock.

The Wyckoff Methodology is based on the concept of "buy low, sell high," so in real estate investing, you will need to buy a property when the price is low, and then you will need to sell that property off when the price of that property goes up. If you sell your home before it goes up in value then you will be able to make a profit, but if you wait too long, then you risk losing money.

The Wyckoff Method is a very simple and straightforward theory. It is a very simple way of making wise investment decisions, and it can effectively work in almost all markets. This is mainly because, when successful, the Wyckoff Methodology will be able to accurately predict real estate's price movements. When it comes to applying this method, there are some successful investors who have actually been using this system since the 1930s. All they did was simply buy low, sell high with any investment, just as you would buy a stock or a piece of land in the real world.

The Wyckoff Method is very effective for those who want to make smart decisions regarding their real estate investments. It is a very good way for an investor to make profits, especially if they are not sure whether or not they should buy or sell given properties. In most cases, if an investor wants to sell off their property, then they would need to determine where the price of that property is headed and then come up with a selling plan based on that particular information.

Many investors make one mistake when using the Wyckoff Method by taking the prices listed on their local real estate market as gospel. The prices that are listed on the local real estate market might look very appealing, but this can be dangerous because it can lead an investor to assume that the price will always be this way. For example, suppose an investor thinks that their neighborhood is going to become more popular in the future because of some upcoming event. In that case, they might assume that they will eventually own a property worth $100,000 or even $200,000. This is not always how real estate markets work, and a very smart investor knows this. If an investor plans to buy up real estate, they should always know exactly how much their property is worth at its current market value.

There are also a lot of wealthy investors around the world who have been using the Wyckoff Methodology for years to buy and sell some of the most expensive pieces of land in the world. They have been able to achieve significant profits just by applying this simple methodology.

The Wyckoff Method is based on supply and demand, and the more demand a piece of land has may mean a higher price for that piece of property if it's in a good location. The Wyckoff Method also focuses on appreciation, and the more a piece of land appreciates in value, the higher a price it will eventually get if there is a high demand for that particular piece of property.

The Wyckoff Methodology also works well when applied to stocks, but of course, there are some different details that you will need to keep in mind if you want to do so. For example, with stocks, you would need to use technical analysis charts and figure out the highs and lows for each stock before you buy or sell off your shares.

Conclusion

"The Wyckoff Method is a logical, scientific approach to understanding and analyzing stock takes. It defines stocks based on the value they create for their shareholders over any given period of time."

Investing can be a challenging concept to understand, especially for those who are not familiar with the market or stock trading. This will take you through a basic explanation of what The Wyckoff Method is and how it works.

The Wyckoff Method is a mathematical way to make money by finding and following trends. It can be applied to any market, and it provides a unique way of looking at the market and analyzing price patterns for any given period. A trading system that can pinpoint appropriate entry and exit points—that's what we call The Wyckoff Method—not only increases your chances of success as a trader it will also enable you to increase your profits as a trader. By using The Wyckoff Method as a tool, you will experience an increase in confidence as well as profits expectations.

- Domain analysis requires the analyst to view the market in terms of its various "domains," which are defined by characteristics common to stocks within each domain. The domains are arranged sequentially according to their capacities for gains or losses. The logic used in analyzing stocks within a particular domain is superior to the analysis of stocks in other domains. In general, the greater the rate of change in price, the more influential the characteristics of that domain will be on the stock price.
- Buying and selling pressure comes from two sources:
    - The money flow from speculators who buy and sell for profit, and
    - The resulting reaction from investors who buy or sell stocks for capital gains or losses.
    - A third source of buying and selling pressure is a reaction to fundamental developments affecting a company's

- financial position, such as earnings reports, mergers and acquisitions announcements, etc.
- The personalities involved in trading a particular stock can be classified as one of five types: floor traders, specialists, market makers, arbitrageurs, and non-directional investors. Each type has a certain way of thinking that can be used to predict his/her behavior.
- When stocks are sold for less than their value to non-directional investors—the "intrinsic value"—their price typically drops toward zero as speculation creates a divergence between the intrinsic value and the current price. This is known as "divergence" or "declining interest," and it results in a decline in share price over time. Divergence can occur at any time and for any reason.
- When the price of a stock rises above its value to non-directional investors, it will inevitably stop rising and reverse itself in a process known as "reversion to the mean." Non-directional investors want to sell when prices rise sharply (for whatever reason) and buy when prices drop (for whatever reason).
- The distance that the price of a stock must travel before it reverts to its mean is referred to as "time." The longer the time, the more time it will take for non-directional investors to buy the stock. The time it takes for shares to revert to their mean price is approximately equal to the space that they must travel above that mean. Once time has elapsed, or space has opened, "non-directional investors" will start buying because they realize that the price has risen above its intrinsic value and should be sold.
- Time can also be viewed as distance in the sense that, while the stock is moving toward its mean, non-directional investors can sit back and watch it come toward them gradually. When other factors, such as rising interest rates warrant a change in their investment outlook, they will be ready to sell.
- Positions held by speculators and arbitrageurs are typically short-term and can be closed out at any time without regard for the position's impact on the stock's long-term trend. Market makers have a longer-term perspective and will gradually close out positions over time, thus influencing the stock price direction to a lesser degree than speculators or arbitrageurs. This concept is

called "trailing" or "running stops."
- When a stock is up, retail investors buy as a result of momentum and investor psychology. Most retail investors do not have the patience needed to wait for the price to re-test its intrinsic value before buying. They buy when they think it's cheap or when they see price movement that makes them act like they are buying. They may over-react when the price hits an important level (e.g., 50% of its mean) but usually sell at some point without regard to the future value of the stock.
- Once you know how to read these trends (i.e., the way that the market prices stocks), you could then set your stop loss lower or take higher profits. Just because a stock is trading above its intrinsic value doesn't mean it can't go up any further. But if it continues to rise, eventually, there will come a time when it will re-test the entire range of its intrinsic value, and this is this point where you make money by betting against the crowd.
- If a stock is up, retail investors start to buy because they think it is cheap. Even if the price does not hit its intrinsic value, many small investors will start buying because they think the stock is going lower and want to get in at a better price.
- The reaction of "non-directional" investors occurs only after the time or distance between a stock's purchase price and its intrinsic value has been established—usually after many weeks or months of gains or losses, and when the majority of speculators have been shaken out of their positions along the way. The fundamental difference between fundamental and technical analysis is that fundamental analysis considers a stock's intrinsic value, while technical analysis determines a stock's price based on how it reacts to fundamental trends.
- A classic example of a correct reading of the trend by non-directional investors is the October 1987 crash in the S&P 500, which began when The Dow Jones Industrial Average started to decline after a short-term rally due to poor earnings reports from US Steel and AT&T Corporation.
- The decline was largely caused by non-directional investors, who had no patience to await the S&P 500 index's intrinsic value re-

testing. What they were reacting to was a sharp decline in the market's underlying value. This relative value shift occurred after the market had already risen by over 100% over the earlier 18 months.

www.ingramcontent.com/pod-product-compliance
Lightning Source LLC
LaVergne TN
LVHW081539060526
838200LV00048B/2148